A MUSICAL PLAY FOR CHILDREN
BY LARRY SHUE

**FROM A STORY BY
HANS CHRISTIAN ANDERSEN**

★

DRAMATISTS
PLAY SERVICE
INC.

MY EMPEROR'S NEW CLOTHES
Copyright © 1985, The Estate of Larry Shue

All Rights Reserved

CAUTION: Professionals and amateurs are hereby warned that performance of MY EMPEROR'S NEW CLOTHES is subject to payment of a royalty. It is fully protected under the copyright laws of the United States of America, and of all countries covered by the International Copyright Union (including the Dominion of Canada and the rest of the British Commonwealth), and of all countries covered by the Pan-American Copyright Convention, the Universal Copyright Convention, the Berne Convention, and of all countries with which the United States has reciprocal copyright relations. All rights, including professional/amateur stage rights, motion picture, recitation, lecturing, public reading, radio broadcasting, television, video or sound recording, all other forms of mechanical or electronic reproduction, such as CD-ROM, CD-I, DVD, information storage and retrieval systems and photocopying, and the rights of translation into foreign languages, are strictly reserved. Particular emphasis is placed upon the matter of readings, permission for which must be secured from the Author's agent in writing.

The English language stock and amateur stage performance rights in the United States, its territories, possessions and Canada for MY EMPEROR'S NEW CLOTHES are controlled exclusively by DRAMATISTS PLAY SERVICE, INC., 440 Park Avenue South, New York, NY 10016. No professional or nonprofessional performance of the Play may be given without obtaining in advance the written permission of DRAMATISTS PLAY SERVICE, INC., and paying the requisite fee.

Inquiries concerning all other rights should be addressed to William Morris Agency, Inc., 1325 Avenue of the Americas, 15th Floor, New York, NY 10019. Attn: Samuel Liff.

SPECIAL NOTE
Anyone receiving permission to produce MY EMPEROR'S NEW CLOTHES is required to give credit to the Author as sole and exclusive Author of the Play on the title page of all programs distributed in connection with performances of the Play and in all instances in which the title of the Play appears for purposes of advertising, publicizing or otherwise exploiting the Play and/or a production thereof. The name of the Author must appear on a separate line, in which no other name appears, immediately beneath the title and in size of type equal to 50% of the size of the largest, most prominent letter used for the title of the Play. No person, firm or entity may receive credit larger or more prominent than that accorded the Author.

MY EMPEROR'S NEW CLOTHES was first presented at Illinois Wesleyan University, in Bloomington, Illinois, in 1968. It was directed by Larry Shue; the costumes were by Sandy Tappen; the set design was by Fred Pierce; the lighting was by Robert Holmer; and the orchestrations were by Chaunce Conklin and Harvey McLellan. The cast was as follows:

FIRST MAN	Bob Asletine (a/k/a Rob Alton)
SECOND MAN	Richard Ticknor
MOTHER	Jane Wynn
LITTLE GIRL	Jayne Malazza
YOUNGER LITTLE GIRL	Trudi Rippi
PONY	Richard Jenkins
PRINCESS	Sharon Jenkins
MR. SKREECH	Joe Gneisen
CLODNEY	Roger Danchik
EMPEROR	Craig Mahlstedt
SCOUT	Carol Frieburg
WEAVER	John Addis

CHARACTERS

FIRST MAN
SECOND MAN
SON
MOTHER
LITTLE GIRL
YOUNGER LITTLE GIRL
PONY
PRINCESS
EMPEROR
SCOUT
SKREECH
CLODNEY
WEAVER
CHORUS OF MEN, WOMEN, BOYS AND GIRLS

SONGS

OVERTURE 5
THE MANGO-CHUTNEY MARCH 8
THE NATIONAL ANTHEM 10
PROCLAMATION! 14
THE BARREL SONG 17
THE ANTAGONIST RAG 23
CALL ME MISTER WONDERFUL 27
MY EMPEROR'S NEW CLOTHES 37
CALL ME MISTER DIRT-FOR-BRAINS 41
THE CHUTNEY CHASE 43
EMPEROR'S EXIT 46
THE BARREL SONG WALTZ 47
FINALE 47

MY EMPEROR'S NEW CLOTHES

The lights come up on the curtained forestage which, we are soon to see, is not a forestage at all but a locality very near the main street of Mango, capital of Mango-Chutney. Mango-Chutney is a small but busily happy kingdom, as exemplified by its Emperor, whose aesthethic inspiration it is to poetically rename every item in his domain, including the Mango-Chutneyites themselves — or the "Lily-pads," as the Emperor occasionally chooses to call them. Unfortunately for us, he has saved the task of renaming himself till last, so for the time being we must know him simply as the Emperor. Mango-Chutney is bounded on the west by the kingdom of Pulmonia, on the north by Bulgravia, on the east by Grebe, and on the south by the Calamine Ocean, and is itself shaped rather like a fish standing on its head. Roughly where the eye of the fish would be, the city of Mango is situated, as well as all the nation's citizens who are really important to us; there are only about eight of them, but they seem to be many more, for as the wonderfully wise Emperor once so cleverly put it, "One Lily-pad in his time plays many parts."

For those to whom such things are important, the time is the present — not, perhaps, the present as we know it, but as everyone knows it should be, before the business of growing up makes him forget. There are certainly no wars. True, the Emperor does maintain an army, but that is because the Emperor puts on a parade every day, and the militia gives it dignity; true, also, that Mango-Chutney has an ancient enemy — Bulgravia — but that is because ancient enemies are always an entertaining topic of conversation, especially if they are your own. Admittedly, Mango-Chutney and Bulgravia did have a war once, before anyone can now remember, but it was unnewsworthy as wars go. The rival armies met on an open field and, having overlooked the necessity of weapons, threw grass at one another for an hour or so, at the end of which time, being exhausted, they sat down, shared some root beer, sang songs, and took a little nap before their worried wives and children came to scold and take them home. But we digress. The time is certainly the present. If you doubt, ask any Lily-pad, and he will affirm the presence of the time.

The lights have been up for at least a moment, and we are anxious for something to happen, but, being visitors to the kingdom, we maintain a polite silence.

Our patience is suddenly rewarded, for we are surprised by anticipatory shouts from the tops of the aisles.

CHORUS. Hurry!
  Hurry! It's time for the parade!
  I don't want to miss the jugglers!
  The parade's about to start!
  Where's Tina? Hurry, Tina, run!
  Will there be clowns and soldiers?
  Will there be candy?
  And dancing girls and ponies?
  How about candy?
  Yes, yes, but hurry!
  Where is the parade?
  Down here, quick!

(*And the townspeople begin to appear, running down the aisles onto the forestage.*)

FIRST MAN. (*Entering* L. *with a wire cart full of peanuts.*) Which way do we go?

SECOND MAN. (*Entering* R.) I'm not sure. Let's look over here! (*They exit* L. *A little girl enters* R. *as a mother and son enter* L.)

SON. Will the Emperor be there today, Mama?

MOTHER. The Emperor is in the parade every day.

SON. I wish I could be Emperor!

MOTHER. Then you'll have to eat your spinach to grow big and strong.

SON. Really? Does the Emperor eat his spinach?

MOTHER. Always. That's how he gets his big, hairy arms and legs. (*She exits* R.)

SON. Gee, it's harder to be an Emperor than I thought. . . . (*Inspiration.*) Maybe I could be a garbageman! (*Running after her.*) Does a garbageman have to—? (*And he is out,* R. *First and second man enter* L., *still with peanut cart.*)

FIRST MAN. That's not where the parade is. That's where the Emperor keeps his horses.
SECOND MAN. Then it must be over here! Hurry! (*They run off,* R. *A younger little girl enters* R.)
YOUNGER LITTLE GIRL. Will the pretty Princess be at the parade?
LITTLE GIRL. As far back as I can remember, she's always been there.
YOUNGER LITTLE GIRL. (*Pirouetting.*) Someday I'm going to be beautiful, just like the Princess!
LITTLE GIRL. (*Leading her* L.) Then you better not eat your spinach.
YOUNGER LITTLE GIRL. Why?
LITTLE GIRL. (*Stopping.*) You want big, hairy arms and legs?
YOUNGER LITTLE GIRL. (*Shocked.*) Uh-uh. . . .
LITTLE GIRL. Well, then—. (*They exit* L. *First and second man enter* R. *The peanut cart is empty, and somewhat mangled.*)
FIRST MAN. That's not the parade either. That's where they keep the elephants.
SECOND MAN. Then it must be through here!
FIRST MAN. Let's go!
SECOND MAN. (*Noticing us for the first time.*) Hey, wait!
FIRST MAN. What?
SECOND MAN. Look!
FIRST MAN. Where?
SECOND MAN. There!
FIRST MAN. Oh, my!
SECOND MAN. Who are they?
FIRST MAN. I don't know. There sure are a lot of them. I hope they're friendly.
SECOND MAN. Me too. (*Attempting to communicate.*) Hello, there. (*But we are shy and do not reciprocate.*)
FIRST MAN. They certainly are quiet.
SECOND MAN. Hello?
FIRST MAN. Never mind them, let's go. (*They turn for a* C. *exit and have parted the curtain just enough for one person to run through, when suddenly one does. He is Pony, the Royal Army, not now looking very disciplined at all, but rather frenzied.*)
PONY. Oh, dear, dear, dear, dear, dear, dear, dear! This is

terrible! I can't find them *anywhere*! Two hundred of them, and I've lost them, and the parade's about to start! Oh, dear!
SECOND MAN. What's the matter?
PONY. (*Too wrapped up in his dilemma to hear.*) I shall probably have my head cut off!
FIRST MAN. Ask him again.
SECOND MAN. What's wrong, Pony?
PONY. Princess Farthingale has told the Emperor to tell me that the parade is *not* to start until the visitors are ready—and I *can't* find the *visitors*!
FIRST MAN. What do they look like?
PONY. According to my briefing, some of them are short, others are tall, some wear glasses, some don't, some wear socks that slip down around their ankles, one has a tooth missing, others chew their nails, some play baseball, others play with dolls . . . and there are two hundred of them! (*The townsmen have been conferring, and decide to venture an opinion.*)
SECOND MAN. Pony, do you think it might be (*Pointing.*) *them*?
PONY. Whom?
FIRST AND SECOND MAN. *Them!*
PONY. (*Seeing us for the first time.*) Oh! Who are they?
SECOND MAN. We don't know.
FIRST MAN. They're very quiet.
PONY. I'll have to check. (*Observing us closely.*) Let's see . . . short, yes . . . tall . . . (*Momentarily stumped.*) glasses, glasses . . . Ah! yes, glasses . . . yes, socks slipping . . . missing tooth, yes . . . baseball. If anyone here plays baseball, please wave, like this. (*We follow his example.*) Good. Dolls. If anyone here likes dolls, clap like this. (*Again we follow.*) Oh, wonderful. Let me get a count. One, two, three,—mmm—*two hundred!* You *are* the visitors! Welcome to Mango-Chutney! But there's no time to lose! The Princess won't let us start the parade without you, so if you're ready, when I count to three, everyone say, "Let the parade begin!" Ready? One . . . two . . . three. Let the parade begin! (*Our response, alas, is too feeble and nothing happens.*) Oh, dear, that wasn't nearly loud enough for the Emperor to hear. He *won't* start until *all* of you are ready, so let's try once more. Ready? One . . . two . . . three! Let the parade begin! (*This time we make a special effort to be heard, and the trick works, for*

the curtain splits to show us Main Street, Mango, and past the cheering crowd march jugglers, acrobats, and Scout, a boy of about twelve. He carries a box on which he makes puppets dance to the brassy opening strains of the "Mango-Chutney March." These attractions move off to be replaced, to even greater cheers, by Princess Farthingale, carried on a litter by four loyal subjects. She is every bit as pretty as a princess should be, but she has spent most of her life chasing butterflies through the castle grounds, and is not so worldly-wise as we; nonetheless she is anxious to learn, and when she needs our help — as she will, upon occasion — we will be only too glad to render it. We know, of course, who has given her the name "Farthingale"; the Emperor likes the sound of the word, though he doesn't know what it means, and thinks it an appropriate name for a princess. And the Princess accepts proudly, placing, as she does, infinite trust in her father's wisdom. She sees us for the first time. She is happy to see us and would wave if that were the courtly thing to do; instead, she whispers to one of her bearers and is let down. She comes forward as the parade continues.)
PRINCESS. Good afternoon, boys and girls! I'm so glad you could visit me here in the kingdom of Mango-Chutney. It's especially nice that you came today, because today we're having a *parade*. But of course, we have a parade every day. My Emperor — my father — I never know which to call him — says to me every morning, (*Imitating him.*) "Harrumph! Princess, this is a beautiful day for a parade. I think I'll have one right now." And he does. You know grownups — some read the paper before leaving for work, others drink coffee — my father needs a parade before he can really get going. Let's watch. (*She turns to the procession, the Mango-Chutney March again welling up. In a trice, Pony appears in his military regalia, marching proudly. He is, we see, the Emperor's army, and we are soon to find that he capably fulfills many other offices as well. He is trying to look dignified, but something about the corners of his mouth and the tilt of his head tell us that he has just made up a riddle for us, and is saving it till after dinner. The Princess turns to us again.*) This is our army. His name is Pony. We never have any wars in Mango-Chutney, so it's not a very *big* army — but it's a very *nice*-looking army, don't you think? I think so. (*Pony exits, and the Princess' look of admiration turns to one of apprehension as the next two marchers appear. Perhaps they are throwing bubble gum to the masses, but if they are we may be sure they would rather be throwing darts, for they are Mister Skreech and Clodney, the Bulgravian ambassadors and sinister villains of the first order. Or perhaps the second or*

third order, for although they are trying very hard to be fearsome, in this land where there is little villainous precedent to work from, they are finding it hard to get the hang of the business. Yet, so earnest are they that sometimes we nearly catch ourselves rooting for their side. Mister Skreech, though slighter, is the leader of the two, and possibly he wears a tall hat to compensate for his lack of physical prowess. It is apparent that Clodney, his apprentice, has always eaten his spinach, and he will threaten to hit any doubter over the head with his club, though at the moment of truth he probably will not hit him, unless by accident. They chuckle darkly and hiss as they pass.) These are two visitors from a kingdom called Bulgravia. I really don't know why, but for some reason I don't feel that I can trust them. They frighten me. I hope they won't do anything bad while they're here. Do you think they will? (*Some of us nod soberly.*) Let's keep an eye on them, then. (*We vow to ourselves to do so, and we watch them like hawks until they disappear. The cheering becomes more enthusiastic, and we are soon to see why. The Emperor himself is about to be carried in on his litter. When he appears he looks pretty much as we have expected. His obvious self-esteem is forgivable since he is a self-made man, and we are gratified to see the royal family properly aware of its regality. The Princess, always encouraged by her father's presence, turns to us happily.*) My father's coming—my Emperor. He's the wisest man in the world. Really. He's read the dictionary *all* the way *through*. And since he knows so many words, he's giving everything and everyone in the kingdom a new name—a *beautiful* name. Isn't that *noble*? (*The appearance of the Emperor is apparently a traditional ethnic song-cue, for the townspeople break into the National Anthem.*)

CHORUS. Mango-Chutney!
  Mango-Chutney!
  Happy women and men!
  If you need a helping hand,
  Simply say the word—
  We will carry your burd-
  Den!

(*The Princess turns to us suddenly, having forgotten to tell us something important.*)

PRINCESS. Oh! I nearly forgot about the salute! When my Emperor gives the Mango-Chutney salute, everybody has to salute with him, like this. (*She places her thumbs in her ears and waves her fingers at us.*) Can everybody do that? (*We do.*) Amaz-

ing! You got it right the first time. It took me years. Now remember to salute when the Emperor salutes. (*He does. We follow. The chorus, also saluting, sings.*)
CHORUS. Mango-Chutney!
   Mango-Chutney!
   Each day's our holiday!
   Won't you come and visit us?
   Hope that you can stay!
   Mango-Chutney!
   Hooray!
(*The hands of the townsfolk are now away from their ears and extended gloriously to the skies, so we stop saluting and wonder whether it is appropriate to applaud a national anthem. Our decision must be quick, for the Mango-Chutney March breaks in again and the Emperor is carried off, the crowd following in his path, leaving us alone with the Princess.*)
PRINCESS. Oh, I love parades! But they're always over too soon, and then I become sad again. Do you know why I'm sad? It's because I am now old enough to be married, but my father says I must marry a prince. I wouldn't *mind* marrying a prince, but there simply aren't any princes around to marry. Oh, there's Prince Humdrum of Pulmonia, but he's only four years old — and Prince Fandango of Grebe, but he's my grandfather. Boys and girls, what shall I do? (*But we have little time to consider her problem, for in comes Pony, still marching, and eminently in control of his forces.*)
PONY. Hup! . . . two . . . three . . . four . . . Hup! . . . two . . . three . . . four! Keep in step, private! Aye, aye, sarge! Hup! . . . two . . . three . . . four! (*Circling the Princess.*) Left . . . *face* . . . two . . . three . . . four! Say hello to the pretty Princess. (*To her.*) How ya doin', pretty Princess? Hup! . . . two . . . three . . . four! Do a dance for the pretty Princess! (*He obediently does so as he counts.*) Hup! . . . two . . . three . . . four! Hup! . . . two . . . three! At ease. (*He smiles at her.*)
PRINCESS. (*Still less than happy.*) Hello.
PONY. Hello.
PRINCESS. You're our army, aren't you?
PONY. Aye, aye, sir! I mean ma'am! And that isn't all I am. I've got lots of other jobs, too. For instance, besides being the Royal Army, I'm the Royal Cook, the Royal Butterfly Collec-

tor, the Royal Secretary, and after every parade I'm the Royal Street Cleaner. My name's Pony. And you're my Princess.
PRINCESS. (*Jolted, but prettily, out of her reverie.*) Your . . . Princess?
PONY. Well . . . I mean, *the* Princess of *my* kingdom.
PRINCESS. Oh.
PONY. (*Noticing her downcast look.*) You're not *sad*, are you? (*Her silence gives her away.*) Tsk, tsk. And on a parade day, too! Why, that's not proper; it's almost—well, I hate to say it, especially to a princess—but it's almost *unpatriotic*. (*She smiles a little, but only to please him.*) You are very pretty, though, even when you're sad. Your hair sparkles like . . . (*Searching for a simile.*) like spaghetti.
PRINCESS. (*Again caught off guard, and not certain she has been complimented.*) *Spaghetti?*
PONY. I *like* spaghetti.
PRINCESS. Oh.
PONY. Okay?
PRINCESS. Okay.
PONY. A princess really shouldn't be sad, you know. What's the matter?
PRINCESS. Well . . . I'm sad because my father won't let me marry anyone who isn't a prince.
PONY. Hm. (*Pacing, thinking hard.*) Are you in *love* with somebody who isn't a prince?
PRINCESS. In love? I don't know—I don't think so.
PONY. Then there's no problem! If you're not in love with someone who *isn't* a prince, all you have to do is find a prince and fall in love with *him*.
PRINCESS. But there aren't any princes, to speak of.
PONY. (*Flabbergasted.*) None?
PRINCESS. Not one.
PONY. (*Temporarily boggled.*) Oh, my. (*They ponder together for a moment.*) Zap! I've got an idea! Maybe you can find an *enchanted* prince, like in the story! A wicked witch turned him into a frog, and all you have to do is kiss him to turn him back into a prince!
PRINCESS. I thought of that. (*She shudders.*) I must have kissed every frog in the kingdom.
PONY. (*Sympathetic.*) No fun, I'll bet.
PRINCESS. You feel pretty silly.

EMPEROR. (*Offstage.*) Pony! (*Entering.*) Where's my army hiding? The young bumbershoot! Pony!
PONY. (*Who has been following him.*) Yes, your highness?
EMPEROR. (*Startled.*) Oh! There you are. Why aren't you ever around when I need you? There's work to be done. You must tell the people about tomorrow's special parade.
PONY. *Special* parade? What's special about it?
EMPEROR. Since in all the world I am the greatest in wisdom, I have decided that from now on my clothes must be the greatest in beauty! And in tomorrow's parade I shall wear my new suit of clothes — the most beautiful suit in the world!
PONY. The most beautiful suit in the world? Wow! I can't wait to see it!
EMPEROR. Neither can I. I haven't got it yet.
PONY. No?
EMPEROR. No. And here's what you must do. Announce a royal contest for all the weavers in the kingdom — whichever one of them weaves the most beautiful suit of clothes will win.
PONY. Aye, aye, sir. And what does the winner get?
EMPEROR. Tell them that the winner can collect half the money in the royal treasury.
PONY. Your highness!
EMPEROR. *If* the winning suit *pleases* me. I say *if* because suits never do please me — rather hot and stuffy, you know. (*Noticing his daughter.*) Oh! Princess Farthingale! Looking very pretty today, child.
PRINCESS. (*Not smiling.*) Thank you, Father.
EMPEROR. (*Perceptively.*) Sad? Now what could be the matter?
PRINCESS. It's the same thing as always, Father. (*Graduating to tears.*) I can't find a prince to marry, and I'm going to be seventy years old before I find one, and whoever heard of a princess seventy years old? (*She sobs.*)
EMPEROR. There, there, my little petit four, don't cry. A prince is bound to turn up soon. (*Her tears continue.*) Please, child . . . (*Getting misty himself.*) don't cry. . . . You know whenever I see you crying (*Sniff.*) I can't help . . . (*Another sniff, then he, too, begins bawling.*) crying myself! (*They continue crying loudly in harmony for several moments.*)
PRINCESS. I can't help crying when I think of my prince!

EMPEROR. (*Also between tears.*) And I can't help crying when I see you cry. (*Suddenly, Pony, too, bursts into tears.*) What are you crying for?
PONY. You're standing on my foot.
EMPEROR. Oh. My sincerest apathy. (*To the Princess.*) At any rate, child, you'll marry when you find a prince, and not before.
PRINCESS. But why must I?
EMPEROR. Because I'm the wisest man in the world—and I know it's the proper thing to do.
PONY. (*Suddenly inspired.*) Your highness—suppose somebody should prove that you aren't the wisest man in the world, after all?
EMPEROR. Don't be silly! I've read the dictionary! I am the wisest person possible.
PONY. But if someone were to show you that you aren't, would you then let the Princess marry whoever she pleases?
EMPEROR. (*Chuckling.*) Me—not the wisest? Ridiculous. Very well, then, Princess, I'll make you a bargain. Proclamation! If any man can prove that I, the Emperor, am not wise by making me believe something is real that is actually not, then I shall give him my daughter, Princess Farthingale.
PRINCESS. A man has to make you believe something is real that is actually not?
EMPEROR. Yes, indeed, he has to (*Music: "Proclamation!"*) Fool me.
PRINCESS. Fool you?
EMPEROR. Fool me!
  If he makes me think a walrus wears a hat—
  If I eat a bowl of mustard, 'cause he makes me think it's custard—.
PRINCESS. Then?
EMPEROR. You belong to him!
PRINCESS. Imagine that!
EMPEROR. All he has to do is fool me!
PONY AND PRINCESS: Fool you?
EMPEROR. Fool me!
  If he tells me that an octopus can fly—
  Or he really makes me think that chameleons are pink—.
PONY AND PRINCESS: Then?
EMPEROR. You are his!

PONY. Oh, really?
EMPEROR. Would I lie?
PRINCESS. (*Spoken.*) Oh, no, Father! You never break a promise.
PONY. It is a promise, then?
EMPEROR. It's a promise! (*Sings.*) Find a man who
   Can make me believe
   That the only sound a cuckoo makes is "*snort*"!
PRINCESS. That your toes are blue and yellow!
PONY. That your head is made of jello!
EMPEROR. That the sea is filled with whipping-cream! In
   short,
   Find a man who can make me think
   A thing that isn't is,
   And the Princess—.
PONY. The Princess—?
EMPEROR. Is his!
PONY AND PRINCESS: Hooray!
EMPEROR. And I'll throw in the other half of the royal treasury—just to make it worth his trouble. (*The Emperor exits.*)
PRINCESS. Nobody could fool my father. Why, he's the smartest man in the world. He's read the dictionary. He knows lots of things.
PONY. (*Who seems to have a message for all of us.*) You can know lots of things and still not be very smart. *We* could do it. (*We discover Scout, skulking toward Pony, eyeing his royal cap.*) Now think hard—how could we fool him? (*Inspired.*) You could dress up in a funny costume and make the Emperor think you're a zebra, or something.
PRINCESS. *Nice* princesses don't do things like that.
PONY. Well, the sooner we think of something, the sooner—. (*Suddenly Scout snatches the cap from Pony's head. Pony pursues him.*) Hey! Come back here! That's the royal helmet! (*He finally corners the boy and grabs the cap.*) I hope you aren't hurt, but you really had no right to take my helmet, you know.
SCOUT. (*Immediately repentant, apologizing hurriedly.*) I'm sorry, but I like it so much, and I see you wearing it in the parade every day, and I thought since you never take it off if I was real careful you'd never know it was gone, but I wasn't and you did and you'll probably have my head cut off and I'm sorry.

PONY. Don't worry, old Scout. As a favor to you I won't cut off your head. But you can't have my helmet. It's my favorite thing in the world, and I won't give it to anyone until something else becomes my favorite thing.
SCOUT. Okay.
PONY. But listen, Scout. I've got an official problem. Want to help me solve it?
SCOUT. Sure. I owe you a favor, anyhow.
PONY. We've got to cheer up the Princess. Stand by. (*Turns to Princess.*) Princess, you are as sad as anybody I've ever seen. But no matter how sad you are, you can't stay sad long if you sing.
PRINCESS. Sing?
PONY. Sing. Ready? Go! (*Directing.*) Ah one, and a two, and a three, and—a four . . . and . . . uh . . . five. . . . What's wrong?
SCOUT. Can't you sing?
PRINCESS. I don't know. I've never learned any songs.
PONY. Oh, that's too bad.
SCOUT. Not so bad. (*Opening his puppet-box.*) I've got lots of songs written down right in here.
PONY. Wonderful! (*He hands her one of them.*) Okay, here we go! Ah one, and a two, and a three, and a four, and . . . a . . . . What's the matter now?
PRINCESS. I can't read.
PONY. Can't *read*?
SCOUT. Not a smidgen?
PONY. Not a dollop?
PRINCESS. Not a garp.
PONY. (*Intensely.*) Scout—conference! (*Aside to Scout.*) This isn't going to be as easy as we thought.
SCOUT. Are we going to need help?
PONY. I think so. (*He turns to us.*) Boys and girls, we've got to get the Princess to sing—but before we can do that we've got to teach her to *read*—but we don't have time to teach her to read whole *words*—we'll be lucky if we can teach her to read letters in the little time we have. Now, how many of you can help me? Who can say the letters of the alphabet? (*Some of us raise our hands with pride in our new knowledge; others of us are more nonchalant, the alphabet being old stuff to us.*) Good. Now if I can remember—a song my grandmother used to sing—it had lots of letters in it,

and numbers—Ah! I remember! It was called "The Barrel Song."

SCOUT. "The Barrel Song"? I've got that right here. (*He emerges from his puppet-box with a large scroll of letters and numbers. It doesn't look like any song we have ever seen, and we are accordingly a bit skeptical.*)

PONY. Let's read it out loud once, before we learn the tune. Then we can teach it to the Princess. Okay? Here we go—one letter at a time. (*We read with him, still not getting the point.*) R – U – M – T – I – C – U – R – I – M – M – T – 2 – N – F – U – R – S – M – T – S – I – O – I – P – T – U. (*We shake our heads in bewilderment, but Pony seems pleased.*) Great. Now I'll sing it once so you can learn the tune. (*Turning to the Princess.*) Princess? Listen carefully, watch the letters, and you'll be singing in no time. (*He sings, as Scout acts out the scene with his puppets.*)

A lovely milkmaid, living all alone
Up on a mountaintop high
Thought of her love who had gone away to war,
With a tear in her eye—

And a barrel was her only friend
As the long, long nights went by.
If you listened very closely then,
You'd hear her cry:

(*He points to each letter as he says it, and they suddenly make sense to us.*)

"R U MT?
I C U R.
I M MT 2.
N F U R S MT S I,
O, I PT U."

(*To us.*) You see how it works? Now this time let's all sing. If we sing loudly, maybe the Princess will sing with us. Ready? (*He sings.*)

Her soldier-boy was marching far away,
Far from the girl that he loved,
And though he fought as bravely as the rest,
She was all he thought of.

As he stopped to rest, he sat down near

Where a wooden barrel lay.
And imagine his surprise to hear
The barrel say:
(*We sing with him as he points again.*)
"R U MT?
I C U R.
I M MT 2.
N F U R S MT S I,
O, I PT U."
(*To us again.*) Look! The Princess is smiling! We can make her keep smiling if everybody sings this time! (*To the Princess.*) Ready, Princess?
PRINCESS. (*Grinning.*) When you are, Pony!
PONY. (*Sings.*) The winter passed, the maiden sadly watched,
And for her soldier she yearned.
Then one day from her window she saw
Her young man had returned.

As she saw him there, her barrel purred—
In her heart it turned to spring.
As she ran to him, the mountains heard
The sweethearts sing:
(*And we join him in the last chorus, as Pony and the Princess, as well as Scout's puppets, take hands.*)
"R U MT?
I C U R.
I M MT 2.
N F U R S MT S I,
O, I PT U.
(*Scout reverses the banner, to reveal more writing.*)
G, U R A QT.
I M 4 U.

U N I
4FR. . . ."
(*As the Princess and Pony skip out, laughing, Pony gives us a secret sign to let us know that he is pleased with us. Only Scout is left. He picks up his puppet-box and begins walking, the curtain closing behind him. Then he hears something, sets his box down, and scurries behind it. Mister*

Skreech and Clodney enter, Clodney with his immense club, which we are hereafter never to see him without. We note also that Mister Skreech has been studying his villainy diligently, for he trills his R's with inimitable expertise.)

SKREECH. The time is ripe! (*Clodney, not looking, runs into him.*) Careful, careful, my brontosaurus! We mustn't bungle this caper.

CLODNEY. What's a caper, Boss?

SKREECH. I'm not sure—but it was one of our spelling words back at villain school, so it must be appropriate. Look around— Be sure no one overhears—. (*Clodney does so, and miraculously manages to brain his master four times in rapid succession. Mister Skreech ends up prone.*)

CLODNEY. Nobody up here, Boss. See anybody in the dirt, there?

SKREECH. Idiot! (*Rising.*) Listen—we must plan carefully if we are to accomplish what we came here to do—(*Horribly evil.*) to steal all the money in the kingdom!

CLODNEY. Cheez. How do we do that, Boss?

SKREECH. The first thing to remember is to keep cool. Now, what do you do if a stranger says hello to you on the street?

CLODNEY. I hit him on the head with my club.

SKREECH. No, no, no! You must never use your club until you can't think of anything else to say or do.

CLODNEY. Oh.

SKREECH. Repeat after me: I will not—

CLODNEY. I will not—

SKREECH. Use my club on anybody—

CLODNEY. Use my club on nobody—

SKREECH. If I can use my brains instead.

CLODNEY. If I can use my brains instead. Gotcha.

SKREECH. Excellent. The next thing you must remember is never to use your real name.

CLODNEY. No?

SKREECH. No. Spies never do. For the moment, your name is—hm—Tabernash.

CLODNEY. Tab—.

SKREECH. Tabernash.

CLODNEY. (*With difficulty.*) Tab-ernash.

SKREECH. Now, pretend I'm a stranger meeting you on the street. (*Assuming the aspect of a happy-go-lucky Lily-pad.*) Ah! Hullo, sirrah!
CLODNEY. (*Nervous.*) Hello.
SKREECH. And what is your name? (*Clodney thinks for several moments, but, alas, he cannot remember. Therewith, true to his vow, he bashes Skreech with his club.*) Lummox! Why did you do that?
CLODNEY. I couldn't think of it.
SKREECH. It's Tabernash!
CLODNEY. Tabernash.
SKREECH. Tabernash. Try again. (*He assumes his role once more.*) Hullo, sirrah! What is your name?
CLODNEY. Tabernash.
SKREECH. Oh, really?
CLODNEY. (*Confused.*) No.
SKREECH. (*Becoming peeved.*) What do you mean, no!
CLODNEY. I . . . uh. . . . (*He is cornered again, and again he bashes his fellow.*)
SKREECH. *How* can you be so stupid, Clodney?
CLODNEY. (*Not about to be fooled again.*) The name's Tabernash.
SKREECH. (*Blowing up.*) No it isn't! From now on I do all the talking; you just keep silent, and don't hit anybody over the head until I tell you to. Very undiplomatic.
CLODNEY. Your command is my wish, Boss. But how we gonna steal all the money in the kingdom if—?
SKREECH. (*Seeing Scout, who has just stepped forward, fascinated by the intrigue unraveling before him.*) Quiet, fool! There's a sniveling little snoop coming our way!
SCOUT. (*Approaching them.*) Hello.
CLODNEY. (*To Scout.*) Quiet, fool! There's a sniveling little snoop coming our way!
SKREECH. (*Aghast.*) Idiot! That *is* the sniveling little snoop!
CLODNEY. (*To Scout, with his best party manners.*) Pleased to meet you, sniveling little snoop; my name's Tabernash.
SCOUT. Oh, really?
CLODNEY. No.
SCOUT. What do you mean, no? (*Cloney thinks for a moment and is on the upswing for his emergency tactic, when Skreech halts his club in midair.*)

SKREECH. (*Aside to Clodney.*) Wait, wait, Clodney, my boy. This young scamp might be of use of us. Let me handle it. (*To Scout.*) Well, well, well, well, good afternoon to you, my little boa constrictor.
SCOUT. Hi.
SKREECH. I wonder if you might be so good as to help us out. My friend and I are a couple of friendly travelers, just passing through your kingdom, and we were wondering if you could show us some points of interest—you know, museums, holidays, royal top secrets—.
SCOUT. (*Admiringly.*) Gee, you spies talk neat.
SKREECH. *Spies!* (*He gestures secretly to Clodney, who begins moving in for the kill.*) Why, my little Tasmanian devil, whatever gave you the idea that we were *spies*?
SCOUT. I heard you say so yourself.
SKREECH. (*Deflated.*) Oh. (*Clodney raises his club to strike.*)
SCOUT. And I'd like to help you.
SKREECH. *What?* (*He sees Clodney, quickly moves between attacker and quarry.*) NO, CLOD—! (*And gives his own much-abused skull to save another's.*) . . . ney.
CLODNEY. Sorry, Boss.
SKREECH. (*Miraculously ignoring Clodney, turning again to Scout.*) You—you'd like to *help* us?
SCOUT. Sure. Why not?
SKREECH. But—but we're horrible and nasty.
SCOUT. I like that in a spy.
SKREECH. (*Taken aback.*) Oh? . . . Well, then, let's get down to business.
SCOUT. Okay.
SKREECH. (*Drooling with anticipation.*) Where can we get our hands on some juicy royal secrets?
SCOUT. I'm not sure. The only royal secrets I know aren't going to be secrets for very long, because Pony is shouting them to everybody in the kingdom.
SKREECH. Anything! Anything!
SCOUT. Well . . . first of all, the Emperor said that if any man could fool him into believing something is real that is actually not, he will give that man his daughter the Princess, and half the money in the royal treasury.
SKREECH. Zounds, Clodney! Do you hear? Half the money

in Mango-Chutney! What a stroke of luck, eh?
CLODNEY. Cheez.
SCOUT. And second, there's a contest tomorrow for all the weavers in the kingdom. If someone gives the Emperor a suit of clothes which is the most beautiful and comfortable in the world and which pleases him greatly, the Emperor will give him the other half of the royal treasury.
SKREECH. (*Aside to Clodney, insane with joy.*) Ods bodkins, Clodney, our fortune is made! All we have to do is, first, figure out some way to fool the Emperor and, second, weave the winning suit of clothes. Then we will have all the money in Mango-Chutney! There must be a way to fool the Emperor! There *must* be! (*Noticing Scout, and producing a gold coin.*) Here's a gold piece for your trouble, my little tarantula. Now, run along.
SCOUT. A gold piece! (*In a quandary.*) No, I'm not supposed to take money from strangers.
SKREECH. But surely we're not strangers!
SCOUT. I don't even know your names.
SKREECH. Skreech is the name, my little hangnail, Laryngitis Plutonius Skreech, Esquire, and this is my apprentice, Clodney.
SCOUT. (*The barrier down, he holds out his hand.*) Hand it over. (*He takes the coin, picks up his box, and runs out.*)
SKREECH. And now to fool the Emperor — and to weave the magic suit!
CLODNEY. Weave? But I ain't ever weaved—.
SKREECH. Quiet! (*Pacing.*) I must think . . . must think.
CLODNEY. . . . think.
SKREECH. The clothes must be more beautiful than anything else in the world. Tell me — what is more beautiful than a cloudy sunset? Or a summer rainbow? Or the glittering trail of a snail on a stone?
CLODNEY. (*After thinking hard.*) . . . nothing.
SKREECH. (*Stumped.*) Hm. You're right. Nothing is—. Wait! That's *it*! Clodney, you're a genius!
CLODNEY. I am?
SKREECH. *Nothing* is more beautiful than those things! *Nothing!* So that's what we give the Emperor to wear in the parade!
CLODNEY. What?
SKREECH. *Nothing!*

CLODNEY. I don't get it.
SKREECH. We show the Emperor a box with nothing in it—and tell him it's full of a special kind of cloth—magic cloth.
CLODNEY. What's supposed to be magic about it?
SKREECH. We say that the cloth is beautiful—that it will easily make the finest suit of clothes in the world—but that anyone who is either stupid or unfit for his job can't *see* the cloth.
CLODNEY. If they're stupid, they can't see the cloth?
SKREECH. Not a cuff, not a stitch, not anything.
CLODNEY. But if there aren't any clothes, the Emperor's gonna think *he's* stupid.
SKREECH. Yes! But will he *tell*?
CLODNEY. Ohh. . . .
SKREECH. Of course not. For that matter, nobody in the kingdom will want his friends to think he's stupid, so they will all pretend to see the clothes.
CLODNEY. Yeh . . . I'm catchin' on!
SKREECH. We will win the suit of clothes contest *and* fool the Emperor and leave with all the money in Mango-Chutney!
CLODNEY. (*Realization growing in his eyes.*) Yeh . . . *yeh!* (*Admiringly.*) Oh, Boss, how can you be such a creep?
SKREECH. (*Suavely.*) Practice, my boy—practice! (*He sings.*)
 Because when
 You know how to be, it's a wow to be ba-ad!
SKREECH AND CLODNEY. Not so great to be, we just hate to be nice! All our lives we've spent acting as bad as we can—.
SKREECH. I was a bad little boy!
CLODNEY. Now you're a bad little man!
SKREECH AND CLODNEY. We think of
 All the money and all the fun we have ha-ad!
 If we ever could, still we never would stop!
SKREECH. We never look both ways when we start crossing the street!
CLODNEY. Put elbows on the table when we sit down to eat!
SKREECH AND CLODNEY. You'll never see us brush our
  teeth or washing our feet!
 Yes, we are ba-ad from tiptoe to top!
SKREECH. (*Speaking over the music.*) Ha-haah! Clodney, my great mountain of jello, our fortune is made! Just think—when we bring him his "new suit"—

SKREECH AND CLODNEY. We'll show him
  Bobs, fandangles, and fobs, and bangles, and bo-ows!
  He'll believe us, and he'll receive a surprise!
  By the time he finds out that he has nothing on,
CLODNEY. He may be angry.
SKREECH. But we will be gone!
SKREECH AND CLODNEY. And when they see His Highness is marching minus his clo-othes,
  Still they'll be bubble-y, love each lovel-y stitch!
CLODNEY. No one will see the clothes no matter how hard he tries!
SKREECH. They'll simply stand there staring, not believing their eyes!
SKREECH AND CLODNEY. They'll walk off feeling dumb, and we'll walk off with the prize!
  Yes, we'll be ba-ad, until we get rich!
  Yes, we'll be ba-ad—
  Untilll—
  We get—
SKREECH. Hold your hat, my boy, soon we're gonna be—
SKREECH AND CLODNEY: Ri-i-i-i-i-i-ich! (*And they are gone. The curtain opens on the throne room of the palace. Various regal trappings combine to make the room the quintessence of opulence. Pony is dutifully sweeping the floor. The Emperor is being measured by a weaver.*)
WEAVER. Raise your arms, Your Highness.
EMPEROR. (*Grumpily.*) "Raise your arms, Your Highness, bend yourself double, Your Highness, stand on your head, Your Highness!" You think I'm an acrobat?
WEAVER. No, Your Highness.
EMPEROR. And don't call me "Your Highness" so much. It gets on my nerves.
WEAVER. Sorry, Your Highness.
EMPEROR. Here it is an hour past my bedtime, and you weaving fellows keep barging in to measure me. I hope you're the last of them?
WEAVER. I really don't know, Your Highness.
EMPEROR. Hm. (*To Pony.*) Oh, Royal Vacuum Cleaner!
PONY. (*Snapping to attention.*) Aye, aye, sir!
EMPEROR. Summon the Royal Army.
PONY. Yessir. (*And he is gone, only to return a second later, march-*

ing.) Hup! . . . two . . . three . . . four . . . Hup! . . . two . . . three . . . four . . . *Companee* . . . halt! (*He stops.*) Royal Army reporting for duty, sir!
EMPEROR. Gentlemen, I want you to surround the palace.
PONY. (*Uncertainly.*) Yessir.
EMPEROR. And when the Royal Secretary comes in, grab him and bring him to me.
PONY. Consider it done, sir! 'Bout . . . *face* . . . two . . . three . . . four . . . Hup! . . . (*And he is out. We hear voices — both Pony's.*) Halt! Who goes there!
 'Tis I, the Royal Secretary!
 Come with us!
 Let go of me!
 We can't! We have our orders!
 Let go, I say! (*Pony pulls himself by force into the room, holding his own arm.*) Hup! . . . two . . . three . . . *halt!* Sir, the Royal Secretary!
EMPEROR. You may release him now. (*Pony lets his arm go.*) Royal secretary!
PONY. Yessir!
EMPEROR. How many more weavers have entered the contest?
PONY. Two more, sir. (*Pulling out a scribbled-up note pad.*) A brother and sister, by the name of Foote.
EMPEROR. And have they arrived?
PONY. Not yet, sir.
EMPEROR. Oh, very well. You've worked hard today — go on home, get some rest.
PONY. (*Who really is exhausted.*) Oh, *thank* you, sir. (*He starts gratefully out.*)
EMPEROR. And on your way out, summon the Royal Cook! (*Pony has exited, and returns just as quickly, as the Royal Cook.*)
PONY. Yessir!
EMPEROR. Have you planned the banquet for tomorrow — after the parade?
PONY. Yessir. We're having boiled pheasant and root beer, sir.
EMPEROR. Ah, delicious! Well, you've done very good work. Go home, get some sleep.
PONY. Gladly, sir! (*He tiredly exits.*)

EMPEROR. Pony! (*Pony stumbles back in.*)
PONY. Yessir!
EMPEROR. You finish sweeping. The floor's a mess.
PONY. Yessir. (*He begins sweeping, presently sweeping himself out the door.*)
EMPEROR. Tell me, weaver—.
WEAVER. Yes, Your Highness?
EMPEROR. What sort of cloth will you use for my suit?
WEAVER. I thought wool might be nice.
EMPEROR. Wool! In the middle of summer!
WEAVER. Well, I—.
EMPEROR. Do you want to *boil* me? Do you want me to melt into a little poodle? Get out! *Out!* (*Weaver hastily exits.*) Oh, dear, twenty weavers in here in the last hour, and not one has come up with an idea that pleases me. Well, I've got one more chance, I suppose. If these last two weavers can't give me a suit I like, I may as well call off the parade. Where are they anyway? Ah, well—while I'm waiting, I'll finish giving new names to everything . . . almost finished. Now, where's my list of words? Does the Princess have it? Princess! (*He exits. Pony reenters, dressed as a bearded old man. It is a wonderful disguise, and at first we do not recognize him. We hear the Emperor from offstage.*) Princess Farthingale! (*The Princess enters.*)
PRINCESS. Yes, Father?
PONY. (*Whispering.*) Psst! Princess!
PRINCESS. Oh! Who are you?
PONY. Sh! It's me—(*He lifts the beard.*) Pony!
PRINCESS. Goodness, it *is* you! I thought you were an old man!
PONY. Good. I fooled you. Now, if I can only fool your father. . . .
PRINCESS. Oh, I see! If you can fool him, I belong to you.
PONY. To me instead of him. And I'll let you marry anybody you want. Oh, sh! Here he comes! (*The Emperor enters. Pony adopts a bent back and broken voice.*) Hel-lo . . . young . . . whipper . . . snap-per.
EMPEROR. Hello, Pony, finished sweeping? (*Pony is tongue-tied.*) Princess, have you seen my list of new names?
PRINCESS. Yes, Father. It's on your bed.

EMPEROR. Jolly good. (*He exits.*)
PRINCESS. (*Disheartened.*) Oh, Pony. . . .
PONY. (*Undaunted.*) Don't worry, Princess! I've got another disguise outside that's even *better*. It'll fool him for sure. Be back before you can do a double somersault! (*He runs out. The Emperor returns with his list.*)
EMPEROR. Here we are, little paramecium. Let's get to work, and maybe we can finish up today, eh? (*Consulting his list.*) Oh! Yes! I'm sure we will! We've only a few things left to name! Let me see . . . hmm . . . "elephant." Now, what would be a good name for an elephant? Ah! I have it! I'll call the elephant a "hose-nose," heh-heh. Yes. And the "rose," lovely flower, deserves a lovely name. I'll call the rose a — a "nifty-sniff"!
PRINCESS. But Father, why are you giving a new name to everything in the kingdom?
EMPEROR. Because, my dear, nothing can be ugly if it has a beautiful name. There's something nice about everything — an elephant's nose, the smell of a rose — and a thing's name should tell everyone how nice it is.
PRINCESS. I'll bet naming everything is fun.
EMPEROR. Oh, it's not so easy as you'd think. Some things are just too *nice* for a name.
PRINCESS. Too nice for a *name*? I can't think of anything like that.
EMPEROR. I can only think of one thing.
PRINCESS. What?
EMPEROR. Me!
PRINCESS. You?
EMPEROR. Yes. That's why naming myself has been the hardest part of all.
PRINCESS. Father! You mean you — ?
EMPEROR. (*Correcting.*) Ah, ah! Don't call me "Father". . . .
(*He sings, suddenly turning into Howard Keel.*)
   Call me
   Mister Wonderful!
   Fall down
   At my feet!
   Praise me to the skies
   Because I'm modest, wise, and neat!

No words
Can describe me,
From "zebra" to "alakazam,"
But call me
Mister Wonderful,
Though it won't describe how wonderful I am!
(*The chorus enters from nowhere.*)
CHORUS. We'll call you
Mister Wonderful!
Fall down
At your feet!
EMPEROR. I'm obstreperous!
CHORUS. Praise you to the skies
Because you're modest, wise, and neat!
EMPEROR. Hermetical!
CHORUS. No words
Can describe you, —
EMPEROR. Pusillanimous!
CHORUS. From Athens to Zanzibar!
EMPEROR. Electromagnetic!
CHORUS. So we'll call you
Mister Wonderful,
Though it won't describe how wonderful you are!
EMPEROR. Each man has a job to do —
Each man has his place —
And mine's a small but useful one —
The leader of the human race!
CHORUS. The word's not
Been invented
That measures
Up to you!
EMPEROR. So till one
Better comes along,
"Mister Wonderful" will simply have to do!
(*They sing in unison:*)

EMPEROR. Call me	CHORUS. Mango-Chutney!
Mister Wonderful!	Mango-Chutney!
Fall down	Happy women and men!
At my feet!	If you need a helping hand
Praise me to the	Simply say the word —

Skies because I'm	We will carry your burd-
Modest, wise, and neat!	Den!
No words	Mango-Chutney!
Can describe me,	Mango-Chutney!
From "zebra" to "alakazam"	Each day's our holiday!
But call me	Why not come and visit us?
Mister Wonderful,	That's what friends are for!
Though it won't describe	Mango-Chutney for
How wonderful	Evermore and evermore!
I am!	Mango-Chutney, hooray!

(*The chorus exits as quickly and mysteriously as it came.*)
EMPEROR. Well, child, like my new name?
PRINCESS. Oh, yes, Father — er, Mister Wonderful. (*We hear a "Psst!" from offstage. The Princess looks in the direction of the sound, and turns excitedly back to her father.*) Oh! We seem to have a visitor! (*Pony enters, dressed in padding, patched trousers, a vest, and a large, black Italianate moustache, and carries an apple.*)
PONY. (*To the Emperor.*) A rivederci, hees-a highness-a. Would-a you like-a nice apple, eh?
EMPEROR. Get some rest tonight, Pony. You're not looking well at all. (*To the Princess.*) Call me if the weavers come, won't you? (*He exits, singing to himself.*) Call me . . . Mister Wonderful. . . . (*And he is out. During the next dejected moment of silence Pony removes his beard. He is out of tricks, and can think of very little to say that is remotely cheerful.*)
PONY. Want an apple?
PRINCESS. Oh, Pony, what are we going to do now?
PONY. I don't know. Whenever I really care for someone, I always let them down.
PRINCESS. You care for me?
PONY. Sure I do, Princess. You know that.
PRINCESS. (*Spunkier than we have ever seen her.*) Well, *I* don't think you've let me down. I think you've been wonderful and brave.
PONY. (*Flattered.*) Aw, no. . . .
PRINCESS. Yes you have. And no matter what happens, I'll never forget you for it. (*Impulsively, she gives him a little kiss. Not so impulsively, he gives her a little kiss. In the midst of the second one, the Emperor enters briefly and sees them without noticing them.*)

EMPEROR. (*Musing absently.*) Little kissing-fish. (*He chuckles and is gone. But not for long.*) WHAAAA! (*He storms back in, on the attack.*) Get out! Ruffian! Out!
PONY. (*As the Emperor backs him out the door.*) But sir—.
EMPEROR. Riffraff! Block! Stone! Begone! (*And Pony is gone.*) And never darken your foot upon my doorstep again! Consider yourself *varnished*!
PRINCESS. (*In tears.*) Oh, Father—. (*She runs out.*)
EMPEROR. (*Following.*) Princess! Please don't cry. I threw him out for your own good. . . . (*He exits. Mister Skreech enters stealthily, disguised only by a pair of glasses.*)
SKREECH. Ah! The coast is clear! (*He looks behind him, and finds Clodney to have fallen behind.*) Clodney! Come in here!
CLODNEY. (*Offstage, reluctantly.*) Aw, Boss, I'd rather not.
SKREECH. What's the matter? Nothing wrong with your disguise, is there?
CLODNEY. . . . I guess not. (*Pleading.*) But *Boss*—.
SKREECH. Then come in! We can't waste time!
CLODNEY. (*Resignedly.*) Ohhh. Okay. (*Clodney enters, wearing a peasant skirt and a blonde female wig. He still carries his club, but it is feminized by the addition of a little pink bow. He carries a hatbox.*) Cheez.
SKREECH. Excellent disguise. Any questions?
CLODNEY. Yeh. Why do I gotta be the lady?
SKREECH. Because I've got to do the talking. Now, should anyone ask, who are you?
CLODNEY. (*Tentatively.*) . . . Tabernash?
SKREECH. No, not Tabernash! You're my sister.
CLODNEY. Your sister.
SKREECH. Perhaps we'd best go over the whole plan once more. Now, what's in the box?
CLODNEY. What box?
SKREECH. (*Pointing, losing his temper.*) *That* box, nincompoop! What's in it?
CLODNEY. (*He sneaks a peek, is about to answer, then quickly looks into it again. Shocked.*) It's *gone*!
SKREECH. *What!* What's gone?
CLODNEY. Whatever was in the box! (*Looking around him.*) Maybe I dropped it coming in.
SKREECH. I'll help you look! (*He joins the search for a moment.*

Then he realizes.) Wait a minute! There was never anything *in* the box!
CLODNEY. There wasn't?
SKREECH. No! Remember? That's the whole trick—to make the Emperor think something is real that is actually not.
CLODNEY. Oh. Yeh. But what if the Emperor—?
SKREECH. Silence! He approaches! Try to look like a lady. (*Clodney strikes an unconvincingly dainty pose as the Emperor enters.*)
EMPEROR. Princess! Where are—? (*He sees them.*) Oh, I say! Who are you?
SKREECH. (*Super-humble.*) Foote's the name, sire, Mister Foote—that's Foote with an *e*—F-double-o-t-e, Foote.
EMPEROR. (*Acknowledging.*) Mister Foote?
SKREECH. And this is my sister—er—Ophelia.
EMPEROR. Ah! Ophelia.
CLODNEY. (*To Skreech, disenchanted.*) *Ophelia Foote?*
EMPEROR. (*Quite taken by Ophelia.*) And a lovely creature she is. Tell me, my pretty little Pumpernickel, why have I never seen such a lovely little flower as you around here before?
CLODNEY. (*Confused.*) Lovely little flower?
EMPEROR. Did anyone ever tell you that you have eyes of emerald . . . teeth of pearl. . . .
CLODNEY. (*Helpfully, pointing to Skreech.*) One time he told me I had a brain of cheese.
EMPEROR. But "Ophelia"—that's no name for a little thing like you. As Emperor of Mango-Chutney, and the wisest man in the world, I am going to give you a *new name*—
CLODNEY. Here we go again.
EMPEROR. —a *beautiful* name. From now on, your name will be . . . *Mimosa!*
SKREECH. (*Repulsed.*) Mimosa?
CLODNEY. Mimosa. (*Touched.*) I like that.
EMPEROR. Sweet little Mimosa.
CLODNEY. (*Really in character now, and giggling.*) Sweet little Mimosa, yeh. . . .
SKREECH. You see, your highness, we came because we heard your Proclamation.
EMPEROR. Proclamation?
SKREECH. About the suit of clothes.
EMPEROR. Oh, yes, that one.

SKREECH. And though we hate to boast, many people say that we are the best weavers in the kingdom.
EMPEROR. (*Impressed.*) Really?
SKREECH. So we said to each other, what a magnificent honor it would be to serve our Emperor, the wisest man alive!
EMPEROR. (*Tickled.*) Yes, you're right. Do you know I'd give the prize in a minute to any weaver who could make me a suit that's comfortable as well as beautiful?
SKREECH. (*Delighted.*) Comfortable! Look no further! You see what Ophelia—
CLODNEY. (*Correcting.*) *Mimosa.*
SKREECH. What Mimosa is holding?
EMPEROR. Yes. . . .
SKREECH. (*With an air of excited mystery.*) It's *enchanted*!
CLODNEY. *Eee!* (*Fearfully, Clodney throws the box down and begins jumping on it.*)
SKREECH. (*Outraged.*) What are you *doing*?
CLODNEY. Run, everybody! The box is enchanted!
SKREECH. No, idiot! (*Shoving him off.*) Get off!
CLODNEY. It's enchanted!
SKREECH. (*Hissing an aside.*) If you say one more word—just *one*—I'll throttle you, Clodney!
CLODNEY. (*In a small voice.*) Mimosa.
SKREECH. (*On the attack.*) *Aargh!*
EMPEROR. (*Breaking up the fight.*) Now, now, tush, tush, friends, let's not squabble, shall we? You were telling me about the box—it's enchanted, is it?
SKREECH. (*Recovering from his rage, though he shoots a lethal glance at Clodney.*) Yes—er, no. Not the box . . . (*He picks it up.*) but what's *inside* the box.
EMPEROR. I say! What is it?
SKREECH. Cloth—for your suit of clothes. *Magic* cloth.
EMPEROR. Magic?
SKREECH. Yes, indeed, sire. It's the most beautiful cloth in the world, and also the most comfortable.
EMPEROR. It's not heavy and hot?
SKREECH. Sire, people who have clothes made of this cloth say that it's so light, they feel as if they have nothing on at all.
EMPEROR. Amazing!
SKREECH. But here's the great thing. The cloth is *invisible* to

anyone who is either unfit for his job or just very stupid.
EMPEROR. (*Astounded.*) You don't say so!
SKREECH. I do say so.
EMPEROR. (*Excited.*) Well, let's have a look, let's have a look!
SKREECH. Ready?
EMPEROR. Oh, yes, hurry! (*Skreech opens the box and daintily pulls out a piece of nothing, about a foot square.*)
SKREECH. (*Smiling more broadly than ever.*) Well? How do you like it?
EMPEROR. (*In an embarrassed aside to us.*) I'll be boffed! I can't see a thing! Not a thing! Can it be that *I* am stupid? Or unfit for my job? I can't let *them* know. I can't let *anyone* know. I'll pretend I can see it. (*Turning to Skreech.*) Oh, yes, you are right! It's lovely. Er, what is it—a hat?
SKREECH. No, sire, it's a handkerchief.
EMPEROR. (*Quickly.*) A handkerchief? Oh, yes, I meant a handkerchief; I said "hat" but I meant "handkerchief." I get them mixed up sometimes.
SKREECH. Yes, sire, I often do that myself. How do you like the color?
EMPEROR. Wonderful! Purple is my favorite color.
SKREECH. It's orange.
EMPEROR. —next to orange, I was going to say, I just love orange. Anyway, it's sort of a purplish-orange, it seems to me.
SKREECH. Perhaps. Did you notice the picture?
EMPEROR. The picture?
SKREECH. In the middle of the handkerchief.
EMPEROR. In the—oh, *yes*, the picture! How could I miss it? Beautiful.
SKREECH. See what it's a picture of?
EMPEROR. (*Nervous.*) Oh, yes, indeed! It's a picture of—uh—.
SKREECH. (*Coaching.*) A . . . picture . . . of. . . .
EMPEROR. A picture of . . . it's a. . . .
SKREECH. A knight.
EMPEROR. A night! Yes, and a lovely night it is, too. There are all the stars, and the moon—.
SKREECH. It's a knight in *armor*.
EMPEROR. Oh, *that* kind of knight, yes—standing *under* the moon.
SKREECH. The sun.

EMPEROR. The sun. (*Anxious to escape this precarious conversation.*) Well, the cloth is wonderful, as you said! Think! A magic suit of clothes! Get to work on it immediately, and I will wear it tomorrow. I'm going to go tell the Princess about it right away!
SKREECH. Yes, sire. Until morning, then?
EMPEROR. Until morning, Mister Foote. (*Chucking Clodney under the chin.*) I trust I'll see *you* tomorrow, my lovely little lily? (*Clodney giggles.*) Very well, then! Work to be done! Trot, trot! (*Exiting.*) Princess! (*He is gone.*)
SKREECH. Ha! The worst is over! Now to spend the night weaving—weaving invisible clothes! (*He starts to go.*) Come along, Clodney. (*But Clodney does not seem to hear him.*) Clodney! (*Clodney still does not react. Begrudgingly.*) MIMOSA! (*Clodney looks up coyly and, humming a little tune, skips daintily out. Skreech follows, shaking his head at his comrade's revolting metamorphosis, as if to say, "What hath the Emperor wrought?" We are quickly taken to the curtained forestage again, on which we see a barrel opposite a little hut in which the weavers sit, their feet propped on the loom, smoking huge cigars. The townspeople are gathered about the hut, excitedly, though vainly, trying to peek through the shuttered windows. Among them is Scout, watching coolly.*)
CHORUS. (*Talking excitedly.*) Can you see them?
  Not at all!
  They must be working hard, to finish the suit!
  Have you seen the cloth?
  No!
  They say it's wonderful!
  Beautiful!
  And magic!
  Whoever is stupid—
  Or unfit for his job—
  Can't *see* the cloth!
  It's invisible!
  Are they in there?
  They've been in there all night!
  If we listen, maybe we can hear them!
(*They become silent.*)
SKREECH. (*Casually leaning back and shouting.*) A little more ruffle on the cuff, sister! Don't forget the fandangles on the

minuet, or the truffles on the sachet! Keep working!
SECOND MAN. (*To the crowd.*) Look! There's an open window over here! (*He points to the space through which we are looking. Skreech leaps up.*)
SKREECH. Quick, sister, the shutter! (*And they close the shutter in our face. Pony enters and walks past the crowd dejectedly, with only a casual glance toward the hut. Scout sees him and joins him on the other side of the stage.*)
SCOUT. Hi, Pony!
PONY. (*Dully.*) Hi, Scout.
SCOUT. Hey, have you seen the magic cloth yet?
PONY. Nope.
SCOUT. I bet it's neat. Something funny about those two weavers, though. I'm sure I've seen them before, but I can't think where. (*Pony does not seem interested.*) Haven't seen the new clothes, huh? (*Pony shakes his head.*) I thought maybe, since you work in the palace and all, you might have gotten a peek at them.
PONY. No. I don't work there anymore.
SCOUT. You don't? Why not?
PONY. I got fired.
SCOUT. Shot down? Really? (*Pony nods.*) I *thought* you looked unhappy. I've never seen you unhappy before.
PONY. Yeah. And hungry too.
SCOUT. No money?
PONY. No.
SCOUT. Well, (*Pulling a coin from his pocket.*) I've got a five-harnen gold piece. Tell you what — I'll give you this, for your hat.
PONY. Forget it. I wouldn't give you this helmet for a hundred gold pieces.
SCOUT. Oh, you would too.
PONY. No, I wouldn't. It's my favorite thing.
SCOUT. But a hundred gold pieces! Think what you could — .
PONY. (*Stolid.*) Nope. Wouldn't do it.
SCOUT. What would you trade it for?
PONY. Something I liked better than this helmet.
SCOUT. (*As if the world were his.*) Name it! I'll get it, somehow. I really want that hat. (*But Pony has sunk into reverie again.*) Pony? . . . Well, anyway, (*He hands him the gold piece.*) here, keep it. I'd

just blow it on lemonade, anyhow. (*Exciting.*) Lotsa luck. (*Scout exits.*)
PONY. (*Shouting after him.*) Hey, thanks for this! (*To himself.*) Oh, boy. . . . I never thought I'd see the day when I needed somebody to cheer *me* up. Maybe if I sing—singing helped the Princess. I'll try it. (*And he sings, slowly.*)
   Her soldier-boy was marching far away,
   Far from the girl that he loved,
   And though he fought as bravely as the rest,
   She was all he thought of.
(*Coincidentally enough, he sits down next to the barrel.*)
   As he stopped to rest he sat down near
   Where a wooden barrel lay.
   And imagine his surprise to hear
   The barrel say . . .
PRINCESS. (*Offstage, singing.*)
   R U MT?
(*Pony looks at the barrel and jumps up with a terrified scream.*)
   I C U R.
(*The Princess appears. Pony sees her and laughs.*)
   I M MT 2.
   N F U R S MT S I,
PONY AND PRINCESS. O, I PT U.
PONY. (*Laughing.*) Gosh, Princess. You scared me to death.
PRINCESS. I'm sorry.
PONY. That's all right, I'm glad you did; I mean I'm glad it was *you* and not—. (*He gestures toward the barrel.*) Hey, what are you doing out so late?
PRINCESS. Looking for you. It's morning already.
PONY. Looking for me? Why?
PRINCESS. I wanted to tell you—remember when we were talking—about being in love?
PONY. Yeah?
PRINCESS. Well, I've been thinking about it, and Pony, I don't think I could *fall* in love with a prince. They're so stuffy. I think I could only fall in love with someone who's funny, and charming, and smart, and handsome, . . .
PONY. (*She is looking right at him, but he still doesn't get the point.*) Wow. Where you gonna *find* a superman like that?

PRINCESS. (*Taking his hand.*) Right here.
PONY. (*Incredibly stupid.*) Here? But there's nobody here, except you and—(*The light!*) uh-oh.
PRINCESS. Oh, Pony. I'd marry *you*, if *you* were a prince.
PONY. (*Touched, and a little confused.*) And I'd marry you if you were a princess.
PRINCESS. (*After a moment.*) I am a princess.
PONY. Yeah . . . well, you know. . . . (*He is saved by the bell—we hear it beginning to strike seven from the town square.*)
PRINCESS. Oh! It's seven o'clock! I've got to get back!
PONY. Meet me after the parade!
PRINCESS. All right. (*She blows him a kiss and runs out.*)
PONY. (*About a barrelsworth happier, as he tosses the coin in the air and snags it with his cap.*) Pow! (*He runs out. Suddenly, Mister Skreech and Clodney burst from the hut with the large suit-box.*)
SKREECH. (*Triumphantly.*) 'Tis finished! The Emperor's magic suit is finished! To the palace! (*Skreech and Clodney scurry out. The chorus members, excited, begin an animated discussion among themselves.*)
SOLO. It's clear! Becca
SOLO. It's here! Danielle
SOLO. The fashion of the year! = Karishia
SOLO. The very latest word in modern dress! Mel F
CHORUS. Yes! (*The music begins.*)
SOLO. To people I've been talking to
 It's even worth the walking to,
 To see his highness's brand new
 Enchanted Sunday suit!
SOLO. It's magical, I understand,   Brittany
 With one enchanted shoulder-band,
 Eighteen enchanted buttons, and
 Enchanted boots, to boot.
SOLO. The enchanted vest is orange,
 And the painter painted four ang-   Celica
 Elic cupids from the collar to the toe!
SOLO. And the clipper of the stitches
 Put a zipper in the britches,   Becca
 And that's enchanted too!
CHORUS. No!

37

SOLO. Yes!
CHORUS. (*Singing.*)
    My Emperor's new clothes!
    My Emperor's new clothes!
    They're magic! If you're stupid as can be—
    Or your job you like to shirk,
    And you're unfit for your work—
    Then there's not a stitch that you can see!

    But that's no concern of mine,
    For I'm sure to see the fine,
    Splendid artistry with which the weavers chose
    The ruffs,
    The cuffs,
    The fur-
    Belows,
    For my Emperor,
    My Emperor's new clothes!

    For the colors they went to
    Blue Hawaii for the blue,
    And they sent away to China for the red,
    And the suit is looked upon
    By the Seamsters' Union
    As a modern masterpiece of thread!

    We'll raise a round of cheers
    When the Emperor appears,
    And he marches through the town and proudly shows
    The fobs,
    The bobs,
    The frills,
    The bows,
    On my Emperor's new clothes!
(*The curtain splits to show the main street again, and the chorus members move into their spectator positions as we hear a few bars of the Mango-Chutney March. They are ajump with anticipation.*)
SOLOS. Oh, boy! Will this parade be great!
    Good heavens, I can hardly wait!
    I hope they don't get started late!

SCOUT. Hey, Snookie, I can't see!
SOLOS. The people are all turning out!
  I'm gonna run and jump and shout!
  What seems to be the problem, Scout?
SCOUT. Hey, Percy, carry me!
(*A man places Scout aloft on his shoulders.*)
SOLOS. I really am excited,
  And I'm sure I'll be delighted
  When his grace selects the moment to appear!
  I can hear the drummers drumming!
  Is he coming?
  Is he coming?
CHORUS. He's coming!
  He's coming!
  He's *here*!
(*And the Emperor appears with a stately pride in his countenance and carriage, and wearing nothing more than an undershirt and a pair of polkadot shorts. The members of the chorus gasp, and each one takes an aside to us.*)
SOLOS. Ods bodkins!
  Impossible!
  I cannot see a shred!
  I cannot see a button!
  I cannot see a thread!
  Can it be that I am stupid?
  Am I unfit for my job?
  Can it be that I'm a nitwit?
  Can it be that I'm a slob?
  I mustn't tell my Emperor!
  I mustn't tell my friend!
CHORUS. I cannot see the clothing, so
  I'll just pretend!
(*The Emperor begins marching proudly about, as the people sing.*)
  My Emperor's new clothes!
  My Emperor's new clothes!
(*The chorus splits into two sections.*)
SECTION 1. His clothes are all in green, I'm glad of that!
SECTION 2. He is all dressed up in red,
  To the hat upon his head!
SECTION 1. And I see he doesn't wear a hat!

CHORUS. Few things can touch my heart
　　Like lovely works of art,
　　But now there's something lovelier than those!
　　From stem
　　To stern,
　　From head
　　To toes—
　　My Emperor's—
　　My Emperor's—
　　My Emperor's
　　New—.
SCOUT. (*With all the innocence of Oliver asking for more.*) But his grace has nothing on!
SOLOS. Ods bodkins!
　　How stupid!
　　Just hear the little fool!
　　The brainless ignoramus!
　　Let's send him back to school!
　　It's clear that he's an idiot!
　　It's clear his mind is gone!
　　What was it that he said?
SCOUT. I said, his grace has nothing on!
CHORUS. His grace has nothing on?
　　His grace has nothing on?
　　Can the child be right in telling us
　　His grace has nothing on?
(*They look at the Emperor and break into a great laugh.*)
SOLOS. It's true!
　　It's true!
　　I knew it all along!
　　There *is* no brand new suit of clothes!
　　His grace has nothing on!
　　Oh, isn't he ridiculous!
　　Most everybody knows
　　That only fools parade around
　　Outdoors without their clothes!
CHORUS. My Emperor's new clothes!
　　My Emperor's new clothes!
　　Can he be just a fool, do you suppose?
　　His clothes

Aren't there!
They're made
Of air!
My Emperor's
New
Clo-othes!
Hah!

(*The chorus exits, laughing and throwing glances full of derogation back at the Emperor. Mister Skreech and Clodney emerge from the shadows, but the Emperor does not at first see them.*)

EMPEROR. Come back, my friends! I can explain! Please come back. . . . I beg you . . . I *order* you to return! I am your Emperor! I . . . am the . . . wisest . . . (*His voice growing weaker.*) the wisest. . . . (*A disheartening revelation that he is not very wise after all.*) Oh, dear.

SKREECH. (*Again affecting Foote's Boston-cream-pie voice and smile.*) Pardon, your highness.

EMPEROR. Hm? (*He sees them, and leaps toward them.*) *You!* You dare show your face before me? The people — *my* people laughed at me; they don't respect me anymore; they'll take my throne away from me, and it's all your doing! You and your suit of clothes! You made me look foolish in front of them!

SKREECH. (*Dodging the Emperor's onslaught.*) Now just a moment, Your Worthiness, I'm certain if we talk it all out, you'll see —.

EMPEROR. Talk all you want — I'm having you arrested in the name of the crown!

SKREECH. Very well, but just listen, for your own good.

EMPEROR. *My* own good!

SKREECH. It's none of *our* business, of course, but would you like your people to call you *unjust* as well as foolish?

EMPEROR. Unjust! I have never been called unjust!

SKREECH. You will be, if you don't keep your promise.

EMPEROR. (*Momentarily baffled.*) My promise?

SKREECH. In your proclamation. Don't you remember? If any man could fool you into believing something was real that was actually not —.

EMPEROR. (*His resolve beginning to topple.*) . . . that something was real. . . .

SKREECH. Such as the suit we gave you —

EMPEROR. (*In a daze.*) . . . the suit. . . .
SKREECH. Then you would give him the Princess and half the money in the kingdom!
EMPEROR. Half the money—. (*Snapping out of it.*) Wait a minute! No! I'm not going to give you anything! You're terrible people! I'm going to put you in prison!
SKREECH. (*Playing it cool.*) All right, then—(*Insinuatingly.*) if you want to be remembered as a promise-breaker. . . .
EMPEROR. What! (*Reflecting, full of anguish.*) No . . . no, that must not happen. . . . The people may think I'm foolish, but I can't break my promise to them . . . I wish I knew what to do. (*To us.*) What should I do? (*But we see no escape from the trap.*) I have no choice. (*He turns back to Skreech, a beaten man.*) Very well, Foote. You've got me trapped. You win. (*He produces a bag of gold.*) Half the money in the kingdom . . . and my daughter the Princess. (*He turns away.*) I'll find her.
SKREECH. (*Relentless, swaggering in his power over the crown.*) Just a moment, Excellency. There's another matter. What about the prize money for the suit of clothes contest?
EMPEROR. (*Pathetic.*) What? But your suit of clothes was just a trick, it wasn't—.
SKREECH. Perhaps, but remember proclaiming that you would give the prize to anyone who gave you a *comfortable* suit?
EMPEROR. Yes, but—.
SKREECH. And was it comfortable?
EMPEROR. Well . . . (*Remembering with a sad little smile.*) yes, it was nice and cool . . . (*Getting hold of himself, firmly.*) but it *didn't* please me. It didn't please me at *all.*
SKREECH. You looked as if it pleased you, when you were marching.
EMPEROR. Well, it didn't.
SKREECH. Oh, *I* believe you, of course, but the question is, will *they*?
EMPEROR. Oh . . . yes. They. (*Giving up.*) All right. All right, talk no more about it—(*Producing another bag.*) take the rest of the kingdom's money. . . . I'll find the Princess. . . . (*Exiting—to himself, nearly in tears.*) The kingdom is ruined . . . ruined.
SKREECH. That's the breaks, old potato. (*The Emperor is gone.*) Ha! Pally!

CLODNEY. (*Ecstatic.*) Boss!
SKREECH. The money is ours!
CLODNEY. I'm so happy! Let's dance!
SKREECH. Not now, you fool! Time is of the essence! We must flee!
EMPEROR. (*Offstage.*) Princess!
CLODNEY. But what about the Princess?
SKREECH. Forget the girl—we have the gold! Up, up, and awa-a-ay! (*And they are gone.*)
EMPEROR. (*Offstage.*) Princess! Where are you? (*The Princess runs in.*)
PRINCESS. Here I am, Father! Where are you? (*Pony and Scout run in from another direction.*)
PONY. Princess Farthingale! There's no time to lose! Which way did those weavers go?
PRINCESS. Why?
PONY. Because they're not weavers at all! They're Mister Skreech and Clodney! They're spies! Scout told me. (*Skreech and Clodney run in through another door.*)
SKREECH. (*To Scout, terribly.*) *Tattletale!*
SCOUT. Help! (*Scout runs out.*)
SKREECH. After him! (*Skreech and Clodney pursue him out.*)
PONY. Not so fast! (*And he joins the chase. The Emperor enters just in time to see Pony.*)
EMPEROR. Pony! I warned you never to return! I'll get you for this! (*He, too, runs out in pursuit.*)
PRINCESS. Father! No! (*She follows, and we find ourselves witnesses to the greatest chase in the history of Mango-Chutney. In and out every door, over walls, under arches run the pursuers and the pursued, a character occasionally lying in ambush for his victim, only to leap out in front of his own predator and reverse direction. The chase becomes more frenzied and widespread, the characters running up and down the aisles as the background music increases in tempo. Finally, on the last measure, Skreech and Clodney barrel in from opposite directions, collide with an earsplitting crash, seem to pause in midair for a lingering moment, and fall as one man, unconscious. The other characters run in from different avenues.*)
EMPEROR. I've got you now, Pony! I warned you never to come back, and now, by Persiflage, you'll pay the price!
PRINCESS. Wait, Father! That's what I've been trying to tell

you — Pony came back to stop those spies from stealing the gold.
EMPEROR. Spies? What spies?
PONY. These two aren't weavers at all. Look! (*He whisks off Skreech's glasses and Clodney's wig.*)
EMPEROR. Mister Skreech and Clodney!
PONY. Some ambassadors, huh?
PRINCESS. Pony's a hero. He saved our kingdom.
EMPEROR. A hero, yes, so you are, Pony. I owe you a most obtuse apology.
PONY. Oh, no, Your Highness, you don't owe me anything . . . but I would be very happy if you let me work for you again — if my job is still open, that is.
EMPEROR. Of course it's open — I couldn't replace you in a century, much less a single day. If I hadn't thrown you out, things might be very different now. (*Gloomily.*) But as it is, I'm afraid I've lost *my* job. My people won't want an Emperor who runs around the streets with nothing on.
PONY. Nonsense! Scout, call the townspeople. Bring them here. (*Scout exits.*)
EMPEROR. Yes, bring them. Bring them here. I might as well turn over my crown to them before they take it from me.
PONY. You might be surprised at what your people think of you.
EMPEROR. No, no, they won't let me be Emperor any more, I'm sure of that. But no matter how badly things turn out, there's one thing I've learned: (*He looks up past us, and as he speaks — even though he still wears his polka-dot undershorts — he seems wiser than ever before.*) That there is no man more foolish than one who parades his wisdom. (*The chorus has begun to enter.*)
PONY. You have plenty of wisdom, sir. You just never knew how to use it before.
EMPEROR. Yes, I've been a silly old man. Ah, if only I had a second chance! (*A crowd has gathered.*) I would be an emperor worthy of the name!
PONY. Maybe you'll get that chance! (*We recognize a twinkle in Pony's eye — the one that means he has a trick under his helmet.*)
EMPEROR. What? (*But Pony has leapt to a platform that raises him above the crowd.*)
PONY. People of Mango-Chutney! I want to talk to you about our Emperor!

CHORUS. (*Scoffing.*) He's no Emperor!
  He's a clown!
  He won't be Emperor long!
  Not of this kingdom!
  We'll see to that!
PONY. Wait! Before you do anything, (*Leaping from the platform and pointing to us.*) let's hear what they have to say! (*To us, pleading.*) Boys and girls, we've *got* to show them that we want the Emperor back! You're the only ones who can save the kingdom now! *Please* — for the Emperor! For the Princess! For me! If you want to save Mango-Chutney, when I count three, yell as loud as you can, "Long live the Emperor!" and salute! One! Two! Three! (*We scream, "Long live the Emperor!" at the top of our lungs and salute so smartly that we hurt our ears, hoping that our fervency has been great enough to convince the townfolk of their error. Pony turns to them.*) You see? Look at them salute! *They* believe in your Emperor! Please say you believe too! People! I beg you! Take back your leader!
CHORUS. (*In quick conference.*) Shall we?
  He's always been a good ruler.
  They believe in him.
  I do too.
  Me too!
  He's the best Emperor we've ever had!
  (*In unison.*) *Long live the Emperor!*
(*They raise the Emperor aloft, cheering wildly.*)
EMPEROR. (*Quieting them.*) Thank you! Thank you. (*To Pony.*) And thank *you*, Pony. Would you like your job back?
PONY. Which one?
EMPEROR. All of them, of course.
PONY. Oh, yes, sir!
EMPEROR. Very well then — (*Asserting his regality once more.*) get to the palace on the double! Clean the moat! Wash the stairs! Trot, trot!
PONY. (*Saluting happily.*) Aye, aye, sir! (*He starts to go, but stops as the Emperor speaks.*)
EMPEROR. And there's one bit of unfinished business! I never break a promise — and I promised to give Princess Farthingale to any man who fooled me.
PRINCESS. But Father, the spies are the ones who fooled you.

EMPEROR. True, but since they do not live in this kingdom, they cannot win a royal contest. Therefore I give her (*Gesturing to his left.*) to *you.*
PONY. To *me?* Oh, *thank* you, sir; how did you know—?
EMPEROR. Not you, ninny! To him! (*He singles out Scout.*)
SCOUT. (*Less pleased than astonished.*) Me?
PRINCESS. Him?
PONY. Scout?
SCOUT. But I'm only twelve years old.
EMPEROR. Nonetheless, it was this boy who first showed me that I had been fooled, when he shouted that I had nothing on. (*Escorting Princess to him.*) I give her to you.
SCOUT. But Your Highness—.
EMPEROR. (*Returning to reclaim his seat on the shoulders of the townsfolk.*) Tush, my boy! Not another word. Your Emperor has spoken!
CHORUS. Long live the Emperor! (*Starting to carry him out with the prisoners in tow, they sing.*) No words
   Can describe you—
EMPEROR. Got to run, now!
CHORUS. From Athens to Zanzibar!
EMPEROR. Always busy, you know!
CHORUS. So we'll call you
   Mister Wonderful—
EMPEROR. To the palace!
CHORUS. Though it won't describe—
EMPEROR. Tallyho!
CHORUS. How wonderful
   You are!

(*And they are gone, leaving Scout and the Princess on one side of the stage and Pony on the other, all three looking a bit dazed and less than happy. As "The Barrel Song" begins playing softly and plaintively in the background, Pony takes a step toward the Princess, and their eyes meet for a moment, but she, as we, is afraid that she will start crying again, and quickly looks at her feet. Pony looks at us for a second, but we have no solution—the Princess belongs to Scout. Pony turns toward the exit, crushed. But suddenly—what's this?—he stops, and turns back. With new hope we see the twinkle return to his eye—he has an idea. He takes off his cap, holds it out toward scout. Scout sees it, nods, and grins. Pony tosses it to him and he promptly dons it. To complete the trade, Scout gives*

the Princess a gentle shove toward Pony. The two take hands. Scout adjusts his hat at a cocky angle and, convinced he has gotten the better end of this bargain, strides out with a wink in our direction. Pony and the Princess, still holding hands, begin to dance as the music swells. The chorus enters, surrounds the dancers, and sings.)
CHORUS. (*In waltz tempo.*) The winter passed, the maiden sadly watched,
And for her soldier she yearned.
Then one day from her window she saw
Her young man had returned.

As she saw him there, her barrel purred —
In her heart it turned to spring.
As she ran to him, the mountains heard
The sweethearts sing . . .

"R U MT?
I C U R.
I M MT 2.
N F U R S MT S I,
O, I PT U!
O, I PT U!
(*And as they repeat the last phrase and end our story, Pony lifts the Princess high above him, never to let her go again, we are sure, and the curtain falls. But the fun is not really done, for the lights come up and the chorus marches back on, singing.*)
CHORUS. My Emperor's new clothes!
My Emperor's new clothes!
They're magic! If you're stupid as can be —
Or your job you like to shirk,
And you're unfit for your work —
Then there's not a stitch that you can see!
(*Scout enters, takes his bow, and sings with them.*)
We'll raise a round of cheers
When the Emperor appears,
And he marches through the town and proudly shows
The fobs!
The bobs!
The frills!
The bows!

On my Emperor's
New clothes!
(*Pony enters, bows, and gestures to the Princess, who joins him as they all sing.*)
R U MT?
I C U R.
I M MT 2!
N F U R S MT S I,
O, I PT U!
(*Mister Screech enters, bows, and gestures gallantly to Clodney, who, still in the guise and character of Mimosa, trips in and curtsies, while everyone sings.*)
Because when
You know how to be, it's a wow to be ba-ad!
If we ever could, still we never would stop!
We never look both ways when we start crossing the street!
Put elbows on the table when we sit down to eat!
You'll never see us brush our teeth or washing our feet!
Yes, we are ba-ad from tiptoe to top!
(*As they begin singing the next reprise, the Emperor himself is carried in on his litter, beaming and singing with them.*)
We'll call you
Mister Wonderful!
Fall down
At your feet!
Praise you to the skies
Because you're modest, wise, and neat!
No words can describe you,
From "Athens" to "Zanzibar,"
So we'll call you
Mister Wonderful,
Though it won't describe how wonderful you are!
(*And everyone, in tableau, salutes and sings.*)
Mango-Chutney!
Mango-Chutney!
Happy women and men!
If you need a helping hand,
Simply say the word!
We will carry your burd-
Den!

Mango-Chutney!
Mango-Chutney!
Each day's our holiday!
Glad that you could visit us!
Wish that you could stay
In Mango-Chutney for
Evermore and evermore!
Mango-Chutney,
Hooray!
(*They are still waving goodbye as the curtain falls.*)

PROP LIST

Wire cart full of peanuts
Identical wire cart, mangled
Box (on which puppets dance)
Soldier and milkmaid puppets
Notepad
Hatbox
Loom
Cigars
Long cord with red, yellow, blue flags
Barrel
Battered hat with white wig glued inside (Pony)

White beard (Pony)
Gold piece
Battered coat
Gnarled cane
Long rope (over 10 ft.)

Black hat (Italian-looking)

Quick black moustache
"Barrel Song" banner
  (with little barrel)

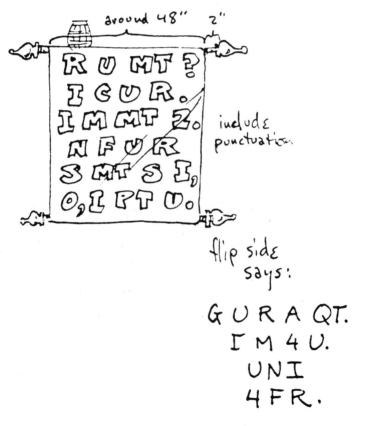

Song sheet
Apple (plastic)
Club
Pink bow for club (detachable)
Peasant skirt (Clodney)
Long blonde wig with pink bow (Clodney)
Cardboard clothes box
Red carpet strip — 17" × 8' (any heavy cloth okay)
Glasses (Skreech disguise)

8 sticks with streamers attached (parade chorus)

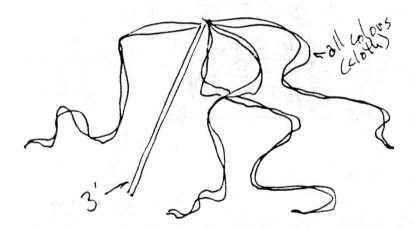

OVERTURE

Overture continued: (i)

Overture continued: (2)

Overture continued: (3)

Overture (continued: (5))

Overture continued: (6)

#1 **THE MANGO-CHUTNEY MARCH**

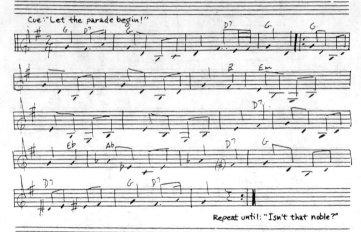

#2 **THE NATIONAL ANTHEM**

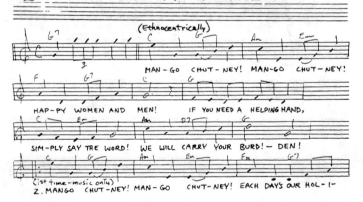

#4 **PROCLAMATION!**

Song is almost entirely spoken. Melody line is for instrumentation.

Cue: (In rhythm) "Yes, indeed, he has to—."

1. (E) Fool me! (PR) Fool you? (E) Fool me! IF HE MAKES ME THINK A WALRUS WEARS A
2. Fool me! (P&P) Fool you? (E) Fool me! IF HE TELLS ME THAT AN OC-TO-PUS CAN

HAT — IF I EAT A BOWL OF MUS-TARD AND HE MAKES ME THINK IT'S CUSTARD (PR) THEN?
FLY — OR HE REAL-LY MAKES ME THINK THAT CHA-ME-LE-ONS ARE PINK (P&P) THEN?

[1st ending] (E) YOU BE-LONG TO HIM! (PR) I-MA-GINE THAT! (E) ALL HE HAS TO DO IS
[2nd ending] (E) YOU ARE HIS! (PR) OH, REALLY? (E) WOULD I LIE? FIND A

RECITATIVE
MAN WHO CAN MAKE ME BE-LIEVE THAT THE ON-LY SOUND A CUCKOO MAKES IS

"SNORT". (PR) THAT YOUR TOES ARE BLUE AND YEL-LOW! (PO) THAT YOUR →

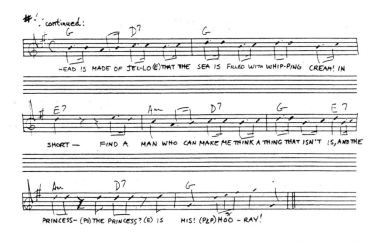

#5 THE BARREL SONG

Cue: "You'll be singing in no time!"

1. A LOVE-LY MILK-MAID, LIVING ALL AL-ONE, UP ON A MOUNTAIN TOP HIGH THOUGHT
2. (HER) SOL-DIER BOY WAS MARCHING FAR A-WAY, FAR FROM THE GIRL THAT HE LOVED. AND
3. (THE) WIN-TER PASSED, THE MAIDEN SADLY WATCHED, AND FOR HER SOLDIER SHE YEARNED. THEN

OF HER LOVE WHO HAD GONE A-WAY TO WAR, WITH A TEAR IN HER EYE. AND A
THOUGH HE FOUGHT AS BRAVELY AS THE REST, SHE WAS ALL HE THOUGHT OF. AS HE
ONE DAY FROM HER WINDOW SHE-E SAW HER YOUNG MAN HAD RE-TURNED. AS SHE

BAR-REL WAS HER ON-LY FRIEND AS THE LONG, LONG NIGHTS WENT BY.   IF YOU
STOPPED TO REST, HE SAT DOWN NEAR WHERE A WOODEN BAR-REL LAY.   AND I'M-
SAW HIM THERE, HER BAR-REL PURRED. IN HER HEART IT TURNED TO SPRING. AS SHE

LIST-ENED VER-Y CLOSE-LY THEN, YOU'D HEAR HER CRY...
AGINE HIS SUR-PRISE TO HEAR THE BAR-REL SAY...
RAN TO HIM, THE MOUNTAINS HEARD THE SWEET-HEARTS SING...

R U M T?   I C U R.   I M M T 2.   N FURS
M T S I, O, I P T U.   U.
Y, U R A Q T. I M 4 U. U N I, 4 F R.

#6 THE ANTAGONIST RAG

cue: "Practice, my boy — practice!"

1. BE-CAUSE WHEN YOU KNOW HOW TO BE, IT'S A WOW TO BE BA-AD!
2. (WE'LL SHOW HIM) BOBS, FANDANGLES, AND FOBS AND BANGLES AND BO-OWS!

(S&C) NOT SO GREAT TO BE, WE JUST HATE TO BE NICE! ALL OUR
HE'LL BELIEVE US, AND HE'LL RE-CEIVE A SUR-PRISE! BY THE

LIVES WE'VE SPENT ACT-ING AS BAD AS WE CAN! (S) I WAS A BAD LIT-TLE BOY!
TIME HE FINDS OUT THAT HE HAS NOTHING ON! (C) HE MAY BE AN-

(C) NOW YOU'RE A BAD LIT-TLE MAN! (S&C) WE THINK OF ALL THE MON-EY AND
-GRY, (S) BUT WE WILL BE GONE! (S&C) AND WHEN THEY SEE HIS HIGHNESS IS

ALL THE FUN WE HAVE HA-AD!   IF WE E-VER COULD,
MARCHING MI-NUS HIS CLO-OTHES!   STILL, THEY'LL BE BUB-BLE-EE,

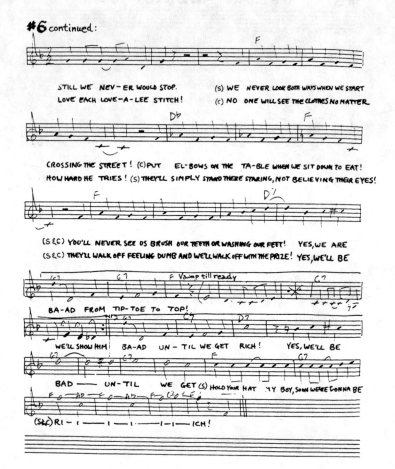

#7 continued:

8 "Barre! Song" reprise - 1 verse & chorus. Cue: "I'll try it!"

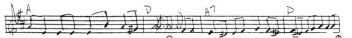

#9 continued: (3)

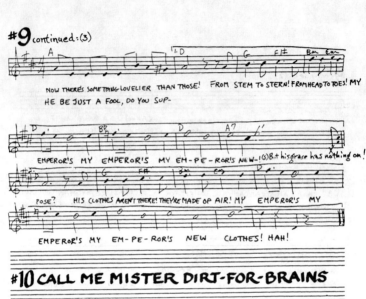

#10 CALL ME MISTER DIRT-FOR-BRAINS

(Dirge) Cue: Segue after applause

#11   THE CHUTNEY CHASE

Cue: "Father! No!" (Play "The Antagonist Rag" 3 times, up-tempo.)

NEW PLAYS

★ **MONTHS ON END by Craig Pospisil.** In comic scenes, one for each month of the year, we follow the intertwined worlds of a circle of friends and family whose lives are poised between happiness and heartbreak. "...a triumph...these twelve vignettes all form crucial pieces in the eternal puzzle known as human relationships, an area in which the playwright displays an assured knowledge that spans deep sorrow to unbounded happiness." –*Ann Arbor News.* "...rings with emotional truth, humor...[an] endearing contemplation on love...entertaining and satisfying." –*Oakland Press.* [5M, 5W] ISBN: 0-8222-1892-5

★ **GOOD THING by Jessica Goldberg.** Brings us into the households of John and Nancy Roy, forty-something high-school guidance counselors whose marriage has been increasingly on the rocks and Dean and Mary, recent graduates struggling to make their way in life. "...a blend of gritty social drama, poetic humor and unsubtle existential contemplation..." –*Variety.* [3M, 3W] ISBN: 0-8222-1869-0

★ **THE DEAD EYE BOY by Angus MacLachlan.** Having fallen in love at their Narcotics Anonymous meeting, Billy and Shirley-Diane are striving to overcome the past together. But their relationship is complicated by the presence of Sorin, Shirley-Diane's fourteen-year-old son, a damaged reminder of her dark past. "...a grim, insightful portrait of an unmoored family..." –*NY Times.* "MacLachlan's play isn't for the squeamish, but then, tragic stories delivered at such an unrelenting fever pitch rarely are." –*Variety.* [1M, 1W, 1 boy] ISBN: 0-8222-1844-5

★ **[SIC] by Melissa James Gibson.** In adjacent apartments three young, ambitious neighbors come together to discuss, flirt, argue, share their dreams and plan their futures with unequal degrees of deep hopefulness and abject despair. "A work...concerned with the sound and power of language..." –*NY Times.* "...a wonderfully original take on urban friendship and the comedy of manners—a *Design for Living* for our times..." –*NY Observer.* [3M, 2W] ISBN: 0-8222-1872-0

★ **LOOKING FOR NORMAL by Jane Anderson.** Roy and Irma's twenty-five-year marriage is thrown into turmoil when Roy confesses that he is actually a woman trapped in a man's body, forcing the couple to wrestle with the meaning of their marriage and the delicate dynamics of family. "Jane Anderson's bittersweet transgender domestic comedy-drama ...is thoughtful and touching and full of wit and wisdom. A real audience pleaser." –*Hollywood Reporter.* [5M, 4W] ISBN: 0-8222-1857-7

★ **ENDPAPERS by Thomas McCormack.** The regal Joshua Maynard, the old and ailing head of a mid-sized, family-owned book-publishing house in New York City, must name a successor. One faction in the house backs a smart, "pragmatic" manager, the other faction a smart, "sensitive" editor and both factions fear what the other's man could do to this house—and to them. "If Kaufman and Hart had undertaken a comedy about the publishing business, they might have written *Endpapers*...a breathlessly fast, funny, and thoughtful comedy ...keeps you amused, guessing, and often surprised...profound in its empathy for the paradoxes of human nature." –*NY Magazine.* [7M, 4W] ISBN: 0-8222-1908-5

★ **THE PAVILION by Craig Wright.** By turns poetic and comic, romantic and philosophical, this play asks old lovers to face the consequences of difficult choices made long ago. "The script's greatest strength lies in the genuineness of its feeling." –*Houston Chronicle.* "Wright's perceptive, gently witty writing makes this familiar situation fresh and thoroughly involving." –*Philadelphia Inquirer.* [2M, 1W (flexible casting)] ISBN: 0-8222-1898-4

DRAMATISTS PLAY SERVICE, INC.
440 Park Avenue South, New York, NY 10016 212-683-8960 Fax 212-213-1539
postmaster@dramatists.com   www.dramatists.com

NEW PLAYS

★ **BE AGGRESSIVE by Annie Weisman.** Vista Del Sol is paradise, sandy beaches, avocado-lined streets. But for seventeen-year-old cheerleader Laura, everything changes when her mother is killed in a car crash, and she embarks on a journey to the Spirit Institute of the South where she can learn "cheer" with Bible belt intensity. "...filled with lingual gymnastics...stylized rapid-fire dialogue..." –*Variety*. "...a new, exciting, and unique voice in the American theatre..." –*BackStage West*. [1M, 4W, extras] ISBN: 0-8222-1894-1

★ **FOUR by Christopher Shinn.** Four people struggle desperately to connect in this quiet, sophisticated, moving drama. "...smart, broken-hearted...Mr. Shinn has a precocious and forgiving sense of how power shifts in the game of sexual pursuit...He promises to be a playwright to reckon with..." –*NY Times*. "A voice emerges from an American place. It's got humor, sadness and a fresh and touching rhythm that tell of the loneliness and secrets of life...[a] poetic, haunting play." –*NY Post*. [3M, 1W] ISBN: 0-8222-1850-X

★ **WONDER OF THE WORLD by David Lindsay-Abaire.** A madcap picaresque involving Niagara Falls, a lonely tour-boat captain, a pair of bickering private detectives and a husband's dirty little secret. "Exceedingly whimsical and playfully wicked. Winning and genial. A top-drawer production." –*NY Times*. "Full frontal lunacy is on display. A most assuredly fresh and hilarious tragicomedy of marital discord run amok...absolutely hysterical..." –*Variety*. [3M, 4W (doubling)] ISBN: 0-8222-1863-1

★ **QED by Peter Parnell.** Nobel Prize-winning physicist and all-around genius Richard Feynman holds forth with captivating wit and wisdom in this fascinating biographical play that originally starred Alan Alda. "QED is a seductive mix of science, human affections, moral courage, and comic eccentricity. It reflects on, among other things, death, the absence of God, travel to an unexplored country, the pleasures of drumming, and the need to know and understand." –*NY Magazine*. "Its rhythms correspond to the way that people—even geniuses—approach and avoid highly emotional issues, and it portrays Feynman with affection and awe." –*The New Yorker*. [1M, 1W] ISBN: 0-8222-1924-7

★ **UNWRAP YOUR CANDY by Doug Wright.** Alternately chilling and hilarious, this deliciously macabre collection of four bedtime tales for adults is guaranteed to keep you awake for nights on end. "Engaging and intellectually satisfying...a treat to watch." –*NY Times*. "Fiendishly clever. Mordantly funny and chilling. Doug Wright teases, freezes and zaps us." –*Village Voice*. "Four bite-size plays that bite back." –*Variety*. [flexible casting] ISBN: 0-8222-1871-2

★ **FURTHER THAN THE FURTHEST THING by Zinnie Harris.** On a remote island in the middle of the Atlantic secrets are buried. When the outside world comes calling, the islanders find their world blown apart from the inside as well as beyond. "Harris winningly produces an intimate and poetic, as well as political, family saga." –*Independent (London)*. "Harris' enthralling adventure of a play marks a departure from stale, well-furrowed theatrical terrain." –*Evening Standard (London)*. [3M, 2W] ISBN: 0-8222-1874-7

★ **THE DESIGNATED MOURNER by Wallace Shawn.** The story of three people living in a country where what sort of books people like to read and how they choose to amuse themselves becomes both firmly personal and unexpectedly entangled with questions of survival. "This is a playwright who does not just tell you what it is like to be arrested at night by goons or to fall morally apart and become an aimless yet weirdly contented ghost yourself. He has the originality to make you feel it." –*Times (London)*. "A fascinating play with beautiful passages of writing..." –*Variety*. [2M, 1W] ISBN: 0-8222-1848-8

DRAMATISTS PLAY SERVICE, INC.
440 Park Avenue South, New York, NY 10016 212-683-8960 Fax 212-213-1539
postmaster@dramatists.com   www.dramatists.com

NEW PLAYS

★ **SHEL'S SHORTS by Shel Silverstein.** Lauded poet, songwriter and author of children's books, the incomparable Shel Silverstein's short plays are deeply infused with the same wicked sense of humor that made him famous. "...[a] childlike honesty and twisted sense of humor." –*Boston Herald.* "...terse dialogue and an absurdity laced with a tang of dread give [*Shel's Shorts*] more than a trace of Samuel Beckett's comic existentialism." –*Boston Phoenix.* [flexible casting] ISBN: 0-8222-1897-6

★ **AN ADULT EVENING OF SHEL SILVERSTEIN by Shel Silverstein.** Welcome to the darkly comic world of Shel Silverstein, a world where nothing is as it seems and where the most innocent conversation can turn menacing in an instant. These ten imaginative plays vary widely in content, but the style is unmistakable. "...[*An Adult Evening*] shows off Silverstein's virtuosic gift for wordplay...[and] sends the audience out...with a clear appreciation of human nature as perverse and laughable." –*NY Times.* [flexible casting] ISBN: 0-8222-1873-9

★ **WHERE'S MY MONEY? by John Patrick Shanley.** A caustic and sardonic vivisection of the institution of marriage, laced with the author's inimitable razor-sharp wit. "...Shanley's gift for acid-laced one-liners and emotionally tumescent exchanges is certainly potent..." –*Variety.* "...lively, smart, occasionally scary and rich in reverse wisdom." –*NY Times.* [3M, 3W] ISBN: 0-8222-1865-8

★ **A FEW STOUT INDIVIDUALS by John Guare.** A wonderfully screwy comedy-drama that figures Ulysses S. Grant in the throes of writing his memoirs, surrounded by a cast of fantastical characters, including the Emperor and Empress of Japan, the opera star Adelina Patti and Mark Twain. "Guare's smarts, passion and creativity skyrocket to awesome heights..." –*Star Ledger.* "...precisely the kind of good new play that you might call an everyday miracle...every minute of it is fresh and newly alive..." –*Village Voice.* [10M, 3W] ISBN: 0-8222-1907-7

★ **BREATH, BOOM by Kia Corthron.** A look at fourteen years in the life of Prix, a Bronx native, from her ruthless girl-gang leadership at sixteen through her coming to maturity at thirty. "...vivid world, believable and eye-opening, a place worthy of a dramatic visit, where no one would want to live but many have to." –*NY Times.* "...rich with humor, terse vernacular strength and gritty detail..." –*Variety.* [1M, 9W] ISBN: 0-8222-1849-6

★ **THE LATE HENRY MOSS by Sam Shepard.** Two antagonistic brothers, Ray and Earl, are brought together after their father, Henry Moss, is found dead in his seedy New Mexico home in this classic Shepard tale. "...His singular gift has been for building mysteries out of the ordinary ingredients of American family life..." –*NY Times.* "...rich moments ...Shepard finds gold." –*LA Times.* [7M, 1W] ISBN: 0-8222-1858-5

★ **THE CARPETBAGGER'S CHILDREN by Horton Foote.** One family's history spanning from the Civil War to WWII is recounted by three sisters in evocative, intertwining monologues. "...bittersweet music—[a] rhapsody of ambivalence...in its modest, garrulous way...theatrically daring." –*The New Yorker.* [3W] ISBN: 0-8222-1843-7

★ **THE NINA VARIATIONS by Steven Dietz.** In this funny, fierce and heartbreaking homage to *The Seagull*, Dietz puts Chekhov's star-crossed lovers in a room and doesn't let them out. "A perfect little jewel of a play..." –*Shepherdstown Chronicle.* "...a delightful revelation of a writer at play; and also an odd, haunting, moving theater piece of lingering beauty." –*Eastside Journal (Seattle).* [1M, 1W (flexible casting)] ISBN: 0-8222-1891-7

DRAMATISTS PLAY SERVICE, INC.
440 Park Avenue South, New York, NY 10016 212-683-8960 Fax 212-213-1539
postmaster@dramatists.com   www.dramatists.com